Notes and Recollections

With *The Historical Setting of the Austrian School of Economics*

∾ LUDWIG VON MISES

Edited and with a Preface by Bettina Bien Greaves

LIBERTY FUND *Indianapolis*

This book is published by Liberty Fund, Inc., a foundation established to encourage study of the ideal of a society of free and responsible individuals.

𒂗𒐆 𒀀𒈬

The cuneiform inscription that serves as our logo and as the design motif for our endpapers is the earliest-known written appearance of the word "freedom" (*amagi*), or "liberty." It is taken from a clay document written about 2300 B.C. in the Sumerian city-state of Lagash.

Front cover photograph of Ludwig von Mises used by permission of the Ludwig von Mises Institute, Auburn, Alabama.
Frontispiece courtesy of Bettina Bien Greaves.

Printed in the United States of America

C   10   9   8   7   6   5   4   3   2   1
P   10   9   8   7   6   5   4   3   2   1

Library of Congress Cataloging-in-Publication Data
Von Mises, Ludwig, 1881–1973.
    Notes and recollections; with, The historical setting of the Austrian school of
    economics / Ludwig Von Mises; edited and with a preface by Bettina Bien
    Greaves.
        pages   cm. — (The Liberty Fund library of the works of Ludwig von Mises)
        Includes bibliographical references and index.
        ISBN 978-0-86597-853-9 (hardcover: alk. paper)—
        ISBN 978-0-86597-855-3 (pbk.: alk. paper)
            1. Von Mises, Ludwig, 1881–1973.   2. Economists—Austria—Biography.
    3. Austrian school of economics.   I. Greaves, Bettina Bien.   II. Von Mises,
    Ludwig, 1881–1973. Notes and recollections.   III. Von Mises, Ludwig, 1881–
    1973. Historical setting of the Austrian school of economics.   IV. Title.
    HB101 .V66A35 2013
    330.15'7—dc23   2013016655

Liberty Fund, Inc.
8335 Allison Pointe Trail, Suite 300
Indianapolis, Indiana 46250-1684

The Liberty Fund Library of the Works of Ludwig von Mises

EDITED BY BETTINA BIEN GREAVES

The Anti-capitalistic Mentality
Bureaucracy
Economic Freedom and Interventionism: An Anthology
    of Articles and Essays
Economic Policy: Thoughts for Today and Tomorrow
Epistemological Problems of Economics
Human Action: A Treatise on Economics
Interventionism: An Economic Analysis
Liberalism: The Classical Tradition
Money, Method, and the Market Process
Nation, State, and Economy: Contributions to the Politics
    and History of Our Time
Notes and Recollections: With The Historical Setting of the
    Austrian School of Economics
Omnipotent Government: The Rise of the Total State and Total War
On the Manipulation of Money and Credit: Three Treatises on
    Trade-Cycle Theory
Planning for Freedom: Let the Market System Work
    A Collection of Essays and Addresses
Socialism: An Economic and Sociological Analysis
Theory and History: An Interpretation of Social and
    Economic Evolution
The Theory of Money and Credit
The Ultimate Foundation of Economic Science: An Essay
    on Method

EDITED BY RICHARD M. EBELING

Selected Writings of Ludwig von Mises

Volume 1: Monetary and Economic Policy Problems Before,
    During, and After the Great War
Volume 2: Between the Two World Wars: Monetary Disorder,
    Interventionism, Socialism, and the Great Depression
Volume 3: The Political Economy of International Reform
    and Reconstruction

LUDWIG VON MISES

CONTENTS

In this book, Liberty Fund has combined two monographs by Ludwig von Mises—*Notes and Recollections* and *The Historical Setting of the Austrian School of Economics*—both dealing with the Austrian School of economics, each from a different perspective. The Austrian School is not a school in the sense of a physical structure constructed of steel, bricks, and mortar. Rather it is a collection of ideas and theories. And it has been called Austrian, because the subjective marginal utility theory of value on which it is based originated largely with Carl Menger, Eugen Böhm-Bawerk, and Ludwig von Mises, all Austrian-born.

Notes and Recollections is a very personal account by Mises describing his life in Austria before he came to the United States in 1940. He wrote these reminiscences in an informal, conversational tone. He wrote of his intellectual development, his effort to understand and explain economic ideas, and his contributions to economic theory, as he himself was then helping to develop it. In these autobiographical recollections he also discussed his activities as adviser to Austrian government officials and his frustrations in attempting to keep inflation and communist and Nazi ideas from destroying the Austrian economy. Professor Sennholz's postscript continues the account of Mises's contributions to the Austrian School of Economics by describing his life and work after he migrated to the United States in 1940.

The Historical Setting of the Austrian School of Economics, first published in 1962, was written in Mises's usual serious writing style. It describes the historical background of the school and summarizes its basic teachings.

When Mises writes in this book of "modern economics," he means economics based on "subjective value marginal-utility theory," which he considered a substantial advance over earlier economic theories. This position set him apart from the classical economists—Adam Smith,

David Ricardo, and John Stuart Mill—who considered economics to be the study of how men produced and distributed material goods and services. As Mises explains in these two works, it also separated him from his German contemporaries—advocates of empiricism, positivism, historicism, and "economic state sciences"—according to whom all knowledge of economics must come from experience and history.

To Mises economics was the study of human action, a science developed logically from the a priori fact that man acts. Economists use reason and logic to explain how men seek to attain their various values, ends, and goals in life—material ends, yes, but also spiritual, cultural, intellectual, social, personal, etc., goals and values. Thus economics is not a physical science. It is a science of reason and logic. It is universal, timeless, and true always and everywhere. The logic of economic theory explains the actions of men in the pre- and post-industrial worlds, as well as in today's highly developed, closely interrelated, world with its finely specialized division of labor. Just as there is no such thing as English mathematics or Chinese physics, the science of economics is the same throughout history, in feudal times as well as in the twenty-first century. Speaking of the Austrian School of economics was a shorthand way to distinguish the subjective value theory developed by Mises's Austrian-born colleagues from the theories of the empirical schools criticized here. In Mises's *Nationaloekonomie* (1940) and *Human Action* (1949), he explained economics in careful detail as the universal science of human action.

The reader should keep in mind that Mises uses "liberal" (derived from the Latin, *liber* meaning free) in its original, classical sense, not in its modern, corrupted definition as interventionism. All numbered footnotes in this edition are mine.

Bettina Bien Greaves
May 2013

Notes and Recollections

FOREWORD

I set out to be a reformer, but only became the historian of decline. —LvM

When my husband, Ludwig von Mises, wrote these words in December 1940, he evidently felt very depressed; but as *Notes and Recollections* indicates, he had not completely despaired about the possibility that the world might yet heed his warnings. Though this book is slim in size, its thoughts are weighty.

The dark mood in which Ludwig von Mises wrote these *Notes and Recollections* is to be understood in part by the circumstances through which they came to life.

On August 2, 1940, my husband and I landed at a pier in New Jersey. We had left Europe in the midst of a bloody, destructive war. Leaving Geneva was not easy for him. He had spent six happy years there, teaching at the Institut Universitaire des Hautes Etudes as Professor of International Economic Relations. He had become well known all over Europe, and the fame of his books had reached the United States well before he set foot on these shores.

The day we arrived in the United States was hot and humid. Behind us were four weeks of traveling, four weeks of anxiety, of heartache and apprehension.* We were admitted on a nonquota visa; but we had no home or family here to greet us. Like many other immigrants, we were to experience difficult times before we once again felt firm ground beneath our feet. Our belongings, among them his valuable library, had been packed and shipped before we left. Now they were lying somewhere en route, and we were not sure that we would ever see them again. Moving from one small hotel to another, with only savings

---

* Cf. chapters V and VI, *My Years with Ludwig von Mises,* by Margit von Mises, Arlington House, New Rochelle, New York, 1976.

to live on, and no teaching position offered that might interest him—such was the background when in the autumn of 1940 my husband sat down to write, as he originally planned, an autobiography.

At the end of December he finished his writing, without having had the benefit of his books for reference. On a bleak December afternoon he showed me the manuscript, and I remember my first impression. I felt immediately, without fully understanding it, that this was a most significant document. But I also realized that it was not an autobiography. An autobiography is the "history of a person's life," Webster says, "written by himself." While this manuscript gives a clear image about my husband's intellectual development, the ideas for his books, his work, and his activities until 1940, it reveals almost nothing about his family or his background.

Two years later, when we finally had an apartment of our own, my husband gave me the handwritten manuscript, which by then was neatly put into two black hardcover folders. "They are yours," he told me, "take good care of them."

Undoubtedly he had written this material for publication. For when I, about thirty years later—when he was recognized all over the world—suggested that he write an autobiography, and offered to type his dictation, he answered: "You have my two handwritten folders. That is all people need to know about me."

It was some time after his death on October 10, 1973, that I remembered the two hardcover folders. I took them out of my closet and read them again and again. I was spellbound. Now I understood what treasure Ludwig von Mises had given me in 1942, when I was not yet ready to see the full historic importance of this manuscript. Never before had he written such candid, harsh, devastating remarks and observations about economic conditions, the universities, the professors, and well-known public personalities in Austria and Germany.

Never before had he expressed such undisguised despair about the coming decline of Western civilization; in retrospect, I would say, he never again wrote in this way. In later years, when his personal situation changed, when he found peace within himself, and when he acquired further insight into the economic conditions and the great possibilities of the United States, he felt a slight hope for the survival of civilization. But never, never would he stop warning against inflation, interventionism, and communism.

I have typed the German manuscript and asked Dr. Hans Sennholz to do the English translation. Dr. Sennholz took his American Doctor of Philosophy degree with Ludwig von Mises at New York University. He is presently Chairman of the Economics Department at Grove City College.

In *Notes and Recollections* the world can hear once again the warning voice of Ludwig von Mises. I hope that many thinking men and women will read this little book. They then will see—and fear—the consequences of inflation, socialism-communism, and the growing power and corruption of interventionist government. History may repeat itself disastrously if we do not change our course.

Margit von Mises
New York, New York
July 1976

I

Historicism

The first source of political and historical knowledge for me was the *Gartenlaube*, the periodical of provincial German folk. This was in 1888, the Three-Kaiser Year; its issues carried reports with many pictures of the lives of the two late Kaisers. I was then not yet seven years old and devoured the articles with insatiable fervor.

A little later I found the historical bias of this family magazine, in more explicit form, in the works of German historians. As an Austrian it was not difficult for me to recognize the political overtones of these writers. And I soon discerned the method of their analysis, which had rudely been called the falsification of history. Nor were the later historians for a united Germany more honest or conscientious; they were merely less capable.

When I graduated from high school, the problems of economic, legal, administrative, and social history appeared more attractive to me than political history. Therefore I decided to study law rather than history, which I earlier had in mind as an undergraduate.

In those years the study of law at Austrian universities was arranged in such a way that three to four semesters of the total of eight were dedicated exclusively to the history of law, and the remaining four to five largely to political economy and public law. The school of law offered greater opportunities for the study of history than the school of liberal arts. The "political" historians who taught at the latter were third- and fourth-rate men. The only significant historian produced by Austria, Heinrich Friedjung, was denied access to an academic career. The emphasis in historical education at the University of Vienna was on paleography.

On Historicism, see appendix at end of this chapter. (All notes that follow are Publisher's Notes, except for original notes which are shown as *Author's Notes*.)

At that time, around 1900, historicism was at the zenith of its career. The historical method was believed to be the only scientific method for the sciences of human action. From the height of his historical clarity, the "historical political economist" was looking with unspeakable disgust on the "orthodox dogmatist." Economic history was the science in fashion. In the German-speaking world [Gustav] Schmoller was adored as the great master of "political economy." And from all over the world ambitious young men flocked to his seminar.

I was still in high school when I noticed a contradiction in the position of the Schmoller circle. On the one hand, they rejected the positivistic demand for a science of law that was to be built from the historical experiences of society; on the other hand, they believed that economic theory was to be abstracted from economic experiences. It was astonishing to me that this contradiction was barely noticed or rarely mentioned.

Another characteristic that displeased me was the school's relativism, which degenerated with many of its adherents to a blind glorification of the past and its institutions. While many progress fanatics had condemned as bad and damnable everything that was old, these pseudo-historians rejected everything that was new, and they glorified the old. At that time I did not yet understand the significance of Liberalism. But to me, the fact alone that Liberalism was an achievement of the eighteenth century, and that it was not known in former times, was no cogent argument against it. I could not understand how they could justify "historically" and "relatively" whatever was in fact tyranny, superstition, and intolerance. To me it was insolent falsification of history to elevate the sexual mores of the past to models for the present. But the worst transgressions occurred in the fields of church and religion, in which Catholics and Protestants alike diligently suppressed that which they did not like. Equally offensive were the writings in Brandenburg-Prussian history, from the "Great" Elector to the "Great" King.

At least in one point the honesty of Austrian law historians differed refreshingly from the bias of Prussian historical work. In his five-hour lecture on Austrian history, which was mandatory for all first-semester students of law, Professor Siegmund Adler dealt with the history of the forgery of the *privilegium majus* by Duke Rudolf, the founder. This was done with such thoroughness that it could withstand the sharpest critique. Only decades later did Ernst Karl Winter find the courage to extenuate this chapter of Austrian history by labeling the late Duke a "socialist" who even exceeded in socialism the idol of German socialists, Kaiser Friedrich Wilhelm I.

It was not quite clear to me how an argument against private property could be derived from the fact that in the distant past there had been community property in land. Nor could I understand why monogamy and family should be abolished because there had been promiscuity in the past. To me such arguments were nothing but nonsense.

On the other hand, I also failed to comprehend the opposite point of view frequently and largely held by the same people: that anything in the course of development was always progress—higher development—and therefore morally justified.

I would here like to mention that the honest relativism of historians searching for knowledge had nothing in common with the mendacious historicism of this school. But logically it rested on no sounder ground. According to its tenets, there was no difference between suitable and unsuitable policy. That which is, is ultimately given. And the wise man who sees things with the eyes of a historian must never judge them, but accept them. They believed that the same was true of the natural scientist, who does not treat natural phenomena any differently.

It does not take many words to prove the fallacy of this position, to which many economists are still adhering today [1940]. It is not the task and function of science to make value judgments. It has one of two functions—in fact, in the belief of many, only one function—to inform us whether the means we apply toward the attainment of an objective are suitable or not. The natural scientist does not judge nature, but informs his fellowmen on which means they should rely in order to achieve certain objectives. The sciences of human action must not judge the ultimate objectives of action, but examine the means and methods that can be applied for the attainment of these objectives.

I frequently discussed this with Ludo Hartmann and later also with Max Weber and Alfred Frances Pribram. All three were rather engrossed in historicism, which made it difficult for them to admit the cogency of my position. With Hartmann and Weber their hot tempers finally prevailed which prompted them to turn to political action in spite of their philosophical doubts. Pribram, who lacked this urge to action, remained faithful to his quietism and agnosticism. One could say about him what Goethe said [*Faust*, second part, *Walpurgisnacht*] about the Sphinx:

Sitzen vor den Pyramiden
Zu der Völker Hochgericht,
Überschwemmung, Krieg und Frieden —
Und verziehen kein Gesicht. *

As for the German historians, I thoroughly disliked their uncouth materialistic position on power. To them power meant bayonets and guns, and realistic policy relied solely upon the military. Everything else was illusion, idealism, and utopianism. They never understood David Hume's famous doctrine that all government rests finally on public "opinion." In this respect their great adversary, Heinrich Friedjung, shared their position. A few months before the outbreak of the Russian Revolution he told me: "I am at a loss when I hear about the mood of the Russian people and the revolutionary ideology that motivates the Russian intelligentsia. That is all so vague and uncertain. Such factors are not decisive. Only the will [to power] of leading statesmen and the plans they decide to execute will count." This differed little from the position of Herr Schober, a petty police official, who later became Chancellor of Austria. Toward the end of 1915 he reported to his superiors that he doubted the possibility of a Russian revolution. "Who, then, could make this revolution? Surely not this Mr. Trotsky, who used to read newspapers in Café Central."

By 1900 the faculty of the University of Vienna had only one instructor who belonged to the German Historical School. Karl Grünberg had worked for a while with Professor [Georg Friedrich] Knapp in Strasbourg, and then published a book that described the agrarian policy of the Austrian government in the Sudetic Mountains. His work slavishly followed in form, presentation, and method, Knapp's book on the old provinces of Prussia. It was neither economic history nor administrative history. It was merely an extract from government documents, a description of policy as found in government reports. Any able government official could easily have written it.

It was Professor Grünberg's ambition to found in Vienna a center for economic history like that created by Knapp in Strasbourg. Knapp's students were then researching the peasant liberation in the several German provinces. And so Professor Grünberg decided that his stu-

---

*   Sitting at the Pyramids
    In the people's highest court,
    Facing flood and war and bustle —
    And moving — not a muscle!

dents should work on the peasant liberation in various parts of Austria. He induced me to work on the history of the lord-peasant relationship in Galicia. As far as possible, I endeavored to free myself from too close an association with Knapp's system. But I succeeded only in part, which made my study, published in 1902, more a history of government measures than economic history.[1] And my second historical work, which I published in 1905, independent of Grünberg—in fact, against his advice—was not much better. Under the title, *A Contribution to Austrian Factory Legislation*, it described older Austrian laws on the limitation of child labor in industry.[2]

While I was spending a great deal of time on these publications, I made plans for more extensive research. It was to be economic and social history but not extracts from official reports. However, I never found opportunity to do this work. After completing my university education I never again had the time for work in archives and libraries.

It was my intense interest in historical knowledge that enabled me to perceive readily the inadequacy of German historicism. It did not deal with scientific problems, but with the glorification and justification of Prussian policies and Prussian authoritarian government. The German universities were state institutions and the instructors were civil servants. The professors were aware of this civil-service status, that is, they saw themselves as servants of the Prussian king. If, on occasion, they used their formal independence to criticize government measures, their criticism was no stronger than the grumbling that could be generally heard in any circle of officers and officials.

Such study of "economic state science" necessarily repelled young people with intelligence and thirst for knowledge. Instead, it strongly attracted simpletons. Indeed, it was not difficult to visit archives and put together a historical thesis from a bundle of official reports. This led to the majority of professorships being held by men who, according to the evaluation yardsticks of independent professions, should be rated as intellectually limited. We must bear this in mind in order to understand how men like Werner Sombart could acquire great reputation. It was necessary, of course, not to be stupid and uncultured.

University instruction in an a priori science presents special prob-

1. *Die Enwicklung der gutsherrlich-bäuerlichen Verhältnisses in Galizien: 1772–1948* (Vienna & Leipzig). Not available in English.
2. *Zur Geschichte der österreichischen Fabriksgesetzgebung (Zeitschrift für Volkswirtschaft, Sozialpolitik und Verwaltung).* No English translation available.

lems if the teacher is to be also a researcher. In any field there are but a few men who can increase the given fund of knowledge. But in the a posteriori experimental sciences both work together—the pioneers and the followers—so that there is no marked distinction between them. In his laboratory, every professor of chemistry can compare himself with the great pioneer. Like him, he is researching even if his contributions to scientific progress are more modest. But it is quite different in philosophy, economics, and in a certain sense also in mathematics. If a professorship were conditional on an independent contribution to economics, scarcely a dozen professors could be found in the whole world. Therefore, if a professorship is to be granted only to independent researchers, work in related fields must also be accepted. Thus, appointment to a professorship in economics would depend on noteworthy distinction in other fields, in the history of thought and doctrine, economic history, especially economic history of the most recent past (which erroneously is called economic problems of the present).

The fiction that in the sciences all professors are equal does not tolerate the existence of two types of professors in economics: those who work independently in economics [as original theorists]; and those who come from economic history and description. The inferiority complex of these "empiricists" gives them a prejudice against theory.

In Germany, and later also in many other countries, this antagonism to theory at first assumed nationalistic overtones. During the first half of the nineteenth century the German professors at best were merely transmitters of the ideas of English economists: only a few, among them Hermann and Mangoldt, should be remembered. The older historical school had a nationalistic resentment against Western [especially English] thought. The younger school then added to the dispute all those arguments with which Nazism rejected Western ideas. To these professors it was a special delight to replace the inadequate English economics with utopian German doctrines. John Stuart Mill was the last Englishman with whom the German professors were still somewhat familiar. He was an epigone of those inadequate Classicists; but, the German professors gave Mill credit for having anticipated some of the great ideas of German economics.

The Historical School of Economic State Science did not produce a single thought. It did not write a single page in the history of sciences. For eighty years it served only diligently to propagandize Nazism. And the thought for this propaganda was adopted, not created. Its historical investigations, which at their best were clumsy data publications, were epistemologically deficient. But the worst aspect of this school was the untruthfulness and conscious dishonesty with which it treated all its investigations. Its writers were always looking "up" for inspiration to their masters in government, turning out dismal partisan literature. Despite their mental limitations, the professors always sought to serve their masters, at first the Hohenzollern family, then the Marxists, and finally Hitler. Werner Sombart expressed their subservience most strikingly when he designated Hitler as the bearer of a divine mandate, for "all authority is from God."

The particular achievement of historicism, namely, the historical theory of the Southwest German School of Philosophy, was the work of other men. Max Weber, the consummator of this work, fought against German pseudo-historicism all his life.

APPENDIX (1978): Historicism

The foregoing critique of Historicism, pertaining to its defective objectives and methods and its lack of integrity, is understandable by itself. For a broader treatment of Historicism, see Mises's *Theory and History* (New Haven, Connecticut: Yale University Press, 1957), ch. 10, pp. 198–239. The first four paragraphs in this chapter (which also has the title, "Historicism") read as follows:

> Historicism developed from the end of the eighteenth century on as a reaction against the social philosophy of rationalism. To the reforms and policies advocated by various authors of the Enlightenment it opposed a program of preservation of existing institutions and, sometimes, even of a return to extinct institutions. Against the postulates of reason it appealed to the authority of tradition and the wisdom of ages gone by. The main target of its critique was the ideas that had inspired the American and the French Revolutions and kindred movements in other countries. Its champions proudly called themselves antirevolutionary and emphasized their rigid conservatism.
>
> But in later years the political orientation of historicism changed. It began to regard capitalism and free trade—both domestic and international—as the foremost evil, and joined hands with the "radical" or "leftist" foes of the market economy, aggressive nationalism on the one hand

and revolutionary socialism on the other. As far as historicism still had actual political importance, it is ancillary to socialism and to nationalism. Its conservatism has almost withered away. It survives only in the doctrines of some religious groups.

People have again and again stressed the congeniality of historicism and artistic and literary romanticism. The analogy is rather superficial. Both movements had in common a taste for the conditions of ages gone by and an extravagant overestimation of old customs and institutions. But this enthusiasm for the past is not the essential feature of historicism. Historicism is first of all an epistemological doctrine and must be viewed as such.

The fundamental thesis of historicism is the proposition that, apart from the natural sciences, mathematics, and logic, there is no knowledge but that provided by history. There is no regularity in the concatenation and sequence of phenomena and events in the sphere of human action. Consequently the attempts to develop a science of economics and to discover economic laws are vain. The only sensible method of dealing with human action, exploits, and institutions is the historical method. The historian traces every phenomenon back to its origins. He depicts the changes going on in human affairs. He approaches his material, the records of the past, without any prepossessions and preconceived ideas. The historian utilizes sometimes, in preliminary, merely technical, and ancillary examination of these sources, the results of the natural sciences, as for instance in determining the age of the material on which a document of disputed authenticity is written. But in his proper field, the exposition of past events, he [the historicist] does not rely upon any other branch of knowledge. The standards and general rules to which he resorts in dealing with the historical material are to be abstracted from this very material. They must not be borrowed from any other source.

II

Etatism

By 1900 practically everyone in the German-speaking countries was either a statist [interventionist] or a state socialist. Capitalism was seen as a bad episode which fortunately had ended forever. The future belonged to the "State." All enterprises suitable for expropriation were to be taken over by the state. All others were to be regulated in a way that would prevent businessmen from exploiting workers and consumers. As the basic laws of economics were totally unknown, the problems resulting from interventionism* could not be foreseen. If they had been foreseen, everyone would have opted for state socialism. However, in ignorance it was left unanswered whether interventionism or state socialism was more desirable.

The program of the Marxian Social Democratic Party† was much

On Etatism, see appendix at end of this chapter.[1]

* On Interventionism, see appendix at the end of this chapter.

† Non-Germans and especially non-European readers will have difficulty correctly understanding the titles of German or Austrian political parties. Dr. von Mises did not consider it helpful to infer from party names, what the parties stood for; his opinion on that score is revealed (in his own words) in his "Tribute to F. A. von Hayek" in Chicago on May 24, 1962, which is presented in an appendix in Margit von Mises's *My Years with Ludwig von Mises*, Arlington House, New Rochelle, New York, 1976, page 183, as follows:

> For centuries the peoples of Europe had longed for liberty and tried to get rid of tyrannical rulers and to establish representative government. All reasonable men asked for the substitution of the rule of law for the arbitrary rule of hereditary princes and oligarchies. This general acceptance of the freedom principle was so firmly rooted that even the Marxian parties were forced to make to it verbal concessions. They called their parties social-democratic parties. This reference to democracy was, of course, mere eye-wash as the Marxian pundits were fully aware of the fact that socialism does not mean freedom of the individual but his complete subjection to the orders of the planning authority. But the millions who voted for the socialist ticket were convinced that the "withering away" of the state meant unrestricted freedom for everybody; and they did not know how to interpret the mystic term "dictatorship of the proletariat."

1. Etatism or statism, a system of government under which individuals are subject to government controls and regulations. Interventionism and socialism are statist systems.

clearer. Marxists theoretically rejected interventionism as mere bourgeois reformism. But, in reality they were themselves promoting a program that embodied a great deal of reformism. Their main field of activity had long shifted to the labor unions, which ignored all doubts raised by Karl Marx and his consistent disciples; and yet they were jealously guarding against any loss of orthodoxy of their master. The Party rejected [Eduard] Bernstein's* attempt to revise the theory and soften the gross contradiction between Marxism and Party policy. However, the victory of the orthodox disciples was not complete. A revisionist group survived, which found expression through the *Socialist Monthly*.

The Social Democratic Party did not arouse the opposition of the middle class on account of the Party's economic program, but because the program was primitive and because it rejected all the facts that did not fit into its socialist scheme of thought. In the Social Democratic Party's scheme of thought:

1. It was a foregone conclusion that capitalism was the root of all evil in the world and that socialism would eradicate it.
2. Alcoholism is a product of alcohol capitalism.
3. War is a product of armament capitalism.
4. Prostitution exists only in capitalist societies.
5. Religion is a cunning invention of priests in order to render working men docile.
6. Only capitalism causes scarcity of economic goods.
7. Socialism will bring unknown riches for all.
8. Nothing, however, excited the opposition of the middle class more than the Social Democratic program of free love.

And yet everyone found a "kernel of truth" in the Social Democratic program. It was found in the demand for social reform and for socialization. All administrations and political parties were animated by Marxian thought. They differed from the Social Democratic Party only inasmuch as they did not think of outright expropriation of all owners and of purely bureaucratic management of all enterprises by the state. Their socialism was not that of Lenin who wanted to organize all industries along the lines of the government postal service. Their so-

---

* On this attempt, see Eugen von Böhm-Bawerk's Chapter 12 in *History and Critique of Interest Theories*, pp. 314–319 (Volume I of *Capital and Interest*); reprinted in the extract, *The Exploitation Theory of Socialism-Communism*, pp. 93–98 (Third Revised Edition, 1975), Libertarian Press, South Holland, Illinois.

cialism was the command system of the Hindenburg Program of the latter part of World War I and of the "German" socialism of Hitler. Private property was to run by orders of government authority. The church socialists wanted to retain a preferential position for the Christian church, and the state socialists one for monarchy and army.

When I entered the university, I, too, was a thorough statist [interventionist]. But in contrast to my fellow students I was consciously anti-Marxian. I knew little of the works of Marx at that time. But I knew the most important writings of [Karl] Kautsky [prominent post-Marxian socialist theoretician]; I was a diligent reader of the *Neue Zeit*; and I had followed the debate among socialists about revisionism of socialism [attempted removal of internal Marxian paradoxes and glaring unrealities] with considerable interest. I was repelled by the staleness of Marxian literature. Kautsky seemed really absurd. When I finally engaged in an intensive study of the important works of Marx, Engels, and Lassalle, I was provoked to contradict them on every page. It seemed incomprehensible to me that this garbled Hegelianism could exert such an enormous influence. I learned only later that the Party Marxists consisted of two groups: (1) those who had never studied Marx, and who knew only a few popular passages from his books; and (2) those who with all the literature in the world had read as self-taught men nothing except the works of Marx. Max Adler, for instance, belonged to the former group; his Marxian knowledge was limited to the few pages in which Marx developed the "super-structure theory." To the latter group belonged especially the East Europeans, who were the ardent ideological leaders of Marxism.

During the course of my life I have met nearly all Marxian theorists of Western and Central Europe. Among them I found only one man who surpassed modest mediocrity. Otto Bauer was the son of a wealthy North Bohemian manufacturer. At Reichenberg high school he had fallen under the charisma of that teacher who almost two decades earlier had introduced Heinrich Heckner to the ideas of social reform. Otto Bauer arrived at the University of Vienna as a devout Marxist. Endowed with indefatigable diligence and quick apprehension, he was well acquainted with the German idealistic philosophy and classical economics. He had exceptionally broad historical knowledge that included also the histories of the Slavic and Oriental nations. In addition, he was well informed on the progress in natural sciences. He was an excellent speaker and could easily and quickly master the most difficult problems. It is true, he was not born to be a pioneer and could not be expected to develop new theories and ideas. But he could have been a statesman, if he had not been a Marxist.

As a young man Otto Bauer had made up his mind never to betray his Marxian conviction, never to yield to reformism or Socialist revisionism, never to become a Millerand* or Miquel.† No one was to surpass him in Marxian zeal. His wife, Helene Gumplowicz, later strengthened him in this resolve to which he remained faithful until the winter of 1918–1919. At that time I succeeded in convincing the couple that a Bolshevist experiment in Austria would have to collapse in short order, perhaps in a few days. Austria depended on the importation of food from abroad, which was made possible only through relief assistance from former enemies. At no time during the first nine months after the Armistice did Vienna have a supply of food for more than eight or nine days. Without lifting a finger, the allies could have forced the surrender of a Bolshevist regime in Vienna. Few people clearly recognized this state of affairs. Everyone was so convinced on the inevitability of the coming of Bolshevism that they were intent merely on securing for themselves a favorable position in the new order. The Catholic Church and its followers, that is, the Christian Social Party, were ready to welcome Bolshevism with the same ardor archbishops and bishops twenty years later welcomed Nazism. Bank directors and big industrialists hoped to earn a good living as "managers" under Bolshevism. A certain Herr Günther, industrial consultant to the *Bodenkreditanstalt,* assured Otto Bauer in my presence that he [Günther] would prefer to serve the people rather than stockholders. One can imagine the effect of such a statement, if it is borne in mind that this man, although mistakenly, was said to be the best industrial manager in Austria.

I knew what was at stake. In a few days Bolshevism in Vienna would have created starvation and terror. Plundering hordes would soon have roamed the streets of Vienna and, in a second blood bath, would have destroyed the remnants of Viennese culture and civilization. Throughout many nights I discussed these problems with the Bauers until I

---

* Alexandre Millerand, born 1859, French socialist, was originally radical; when in power, he limited his activities to moderate programs.

† John von Miquel, 1821–1901, German statesman, originally was an extreme revolutionary; later he was described as one who had entirely surrendered his radicalism, and aimed only at "practical measures for improving the condition of the people irrespective of the party programs."

finally succeeded in convincing them. The resulting restraint of Bauer determined the course of events in Vienna.

Otto Bauer was too intelligent not to realize that I was right. But he could never forgive me for having made him take the position of a Millerand. The attacks of his fellow Bolsheviks especially hurt him. However, he directed his passionate hatred not against his opponents, but against me. He endeavored to destroy me by inciting chauvinist professors and students against me. But his scheme failed. From that time on I never again spoke with the Bauers. Eventually it turned out that I had always had a too favorable opinion of his character; when, during the civil disorders in February 1934, Secretary Fay announced on the radio that Otto Bauer had deserted the fighting working men and had fled abroad with Party funds, I was inclined to consider the statement to be slanderous. I had previously never believed him capable of such cowardice.

During the first two semesters as a university student I belonged to the *Sozialwissenschaftlicher Bildungsverein* (Association for Education in the Social Sciences). Students who were interested in economic and social problems as well as some older gentlemen who sought contact with students, belonged to this Association. Its chairman was Michael Hainisch, who later became President of Austria. Its members came from all political parties. The historians Ludo Hartmann and Kurt Kaser frequently attended the discussions. Among Social Democratic leaders, Karl Renner showed special interest in the Association. Of all the student members, I recall especially Otto Weininger and Friedrich Otto Hertz. In my third semester my interest in the Association began to wane—it took too much of my time.

With great fervor I threw myself into the study of economics and social policy. Initially, I devoured without much criticism all the writings of the social reformers. When a social measure had failed to achieve the desired result, the reason could only be that it was not radical enough. In liberalism, which rejected social reform, I perceived an obsolete world view that was to be opposed vigorously.

My first doubts about the excellence of interventionism came to me when, in my fifth semester, Professor Philippovich induced me to research housing conditions and when, in the following semester in the Seminar on Criminal Law, Professor Löffler asked me to research the changes in law regarding domestic servants, who at that time were still subject to corporal punishment by their employers. It then dawned on me that all real improvements in the conditions of the working classes were the result of capitalism; and that social laws frequently brought about the very opposite of what the legislation was intended to achieve.

It was only after further study of economics that the true nature of interventionism was revealed to me.

In 1908 I joined the Central Association for Housing Reform. It was an Association of all those who sought to improve the unsatisfactory housing conditions in Austria. I was soon appointed reviewer of the pending reform of real estate taxation, succeeding Professor Robert Mayer who had been appointed Minister of Finance.

The undesirable housing conditions in Austria were caused by the fact that taxation discouraged large capital investments and inhibited entrepreneurship in the field of housing. Austria was a country without beneficial land and housing entrepreneurship and speculation. Exorbitant taxation of corporations and high tax rates on capital gains kept men with capital from entering the housing market. In order to provide relief, it would be necessary to reduce the taxes on corporations and on capital gains. But there was no chance for that; the hatred against large-scale capital and against speculation had become too ingrained.

The tax rates on returns from real estate, too, were exceptionally high. In Vienna more than 40% of the gross return was claimed and collected as federal, state, and local taxes. House owners and building contractors strongly opposed this taxation, as it was generally held to be responsible for the high rents. Most owners were small businessmen who invested their savings in a house which savings banks financed at 50% of a customarily over-appraised valuation. The contractors, mostly working with little capital, built either on order by these house owners, or for their own accounts, hoping to sell the finished house as soon as possible. Both groups, owners and construction people, had strong political influence through which they hoped to achieve a considerable reduction in mortgage rates.

A reduction of taxes on housing and land returns would not have reduced the rents. But it would have raised the returns and market prices of real estate accordingly. And in order to compensate for a loss of revenue, the government would have to seek other tax income as a substitute. In other words, such a reform would call for new taxes on others to compensate for tax reductions to landlords.

It was not easy to find general acceptance for my views. At first my report met with misgivings even with the finance committee of the Central Association. But full success soon followed.

My work with the Central Association remained rather intensive until the outbreak of World War I. It offered me great satisfaction. Besides Robert Mayer there were many other excellent economists, such as the brothers Karl and Ewald Pribram, Emil von Fürth, Paul Schwarz, Emil Perels, and Rudolf Maresch.

Only in one point did I differ continually from the opinions of my colleagues. The Central Association was connected with a Kaiser Franz Joseph Anniversary Foundation for Public Housing that was endowed with large funds for housing. These funds also financed the construction of two projects that were to house bachelors. I considered this construction superfluous. Young men in low-income brackets customarily lived with families as sub-tenants. But such close relationships were thought to involve morality dangers. I differed from this opinion, remembering my experience as a field worker during my investigations for Professors Philippovich and Löffler mentioned in the foregoing. It is true, such close associations occasionally led to intimate relationships, but usually they ended in marriage. An investigation by the Viennese moral squad revealed that very few girls under supervision named as their original seducer a "lodger" or "sleeper." But an experienced police official called bachelor housing breeding places for homosexuality. Therefore I considered it an erroneous appropriation to finance such projects out of the available funds.

My view did not prevail. But it was of little consequence, as the war halted all further construction of such buildings. In one of them Adolf Hitler lived at that time.

APPENDIX (1978): Etatism

The full significance ascribed by Ludwig von Mises to the importance and meaning of what he calls "Etatism" appears in Chapter III in Mises's *Omnipotent Government*, Yale University Press, New Haven, Connecticut, 1944, pages 44–78. Representative statements follow (side headings supplied as a reader's help):

> [Importance, page 44] The most important event in the history of the last hundred years is the displacement of liberalism by étatism. Etatism appears in two forms: socialism and interventionism. Both have in common the goal of subordinating the individual unconditionally to the state, the social apparatus of compulsion and coercion.

[Definition, pages 44–45] Etatism assigns to the state the task of guiding the citizens and of holding them in tutelage. It aims at restricting the individual's freedom to act. It seeks to mold his destiny and to vest all initiative in the government alone. It came into Germany from the West. Saint Simon, Owen, Fourier, Pecqueur, Sismondi, Auguste Comte laid its foundations. Lorenz von Stein was the first author to bring the Germans comprehensive information concerning these new doctrines. The appearance in 1842 of the first edition of his book, *Socialism and Communism in Present-Day France*, was the most important event in pre-Marxian German socialism. The elements of government interference with business, labor legislation, and trade-unionism also reached Germany from the West. In America Frederick List became familiar with the protectionist theories of Alexander Hamilton.

[Etatism Attack on Capitalism, page 45] . . . The social scientists outdid each other in emotional criticism of British free trade and laissez faire; the philosophers disparaged the "stock-jobber" ethics of utilitarianism, the superficiality of enlightenment, and the negativity of the notion of liberty; the lawyers demonstrated the paradox of democratic and parliamentary institutions; and the historians dealt with the moral and political decay of France and of Great Britain. On the other hand, the students were taught to admire the "social kingdom of the Hohenzollerns" from Frederick William I, the "noble socialist," to William I, the great Kaiser of social security and labor legislation. The Social Democrats despised Western "plutodemocracy" and "pseudo-liberty" and ridiculed the teachings of "bourgeois economics."

[Socialist Etatism, page 51] Socialism aims at a social system based on public ownership of the means of production. In a socialist community all material resources are owned and operated by the government. This implies that the government is the only employer, and that no one can consume more than the government allots to him. The term "state socialism" is pleonastic; socialism is necessarily always state socialism. Planning is nowadays a popular synonym for socialism. Until 1917 communism and socialism were usually used as synonyms. The fundamental document of Marxian socialism, which all socialist parties united in the different International Working Men's Associations considered and still consider the eternal and unalterable gospel of socialism, is entitled the *Communist Manifesto*. Since the ascendancy of Russian Bolshevism most people differentiate between communism and socialism. But this differentiation refers only to political tactics. Present-day communists and socialists disagree only in respect to the methods to be applied for the achievement of ends which are common to both.

[Interventionist Etatism, page 58] All civilizations have up to now been based on private ownership of the means of production. In the past, civilization and private ownership have been linked together. If history could teach us anything, it would be that private property is inextricably linked with civilization.

Governments have always looked askance at private property. Governments are never liberal from inclination. It is in the nature of the men handling the apparatus of compulsion and coercion to overrate its power to work, and to strive at subduing all spheres of human life to its immediate influence. Etatism is the occupational disease of rulers, warriors, and civil servants. Governments become liberal only when forced to by the citizens.

From time immemorial governments have been eager to interfere with the working of the market mechanism. Their endeavors have never attained the ends sought. People used to attribute these failures to the inefficacy of the measures applied and to the leniency of their enforcement. What was wanted, they thought, was more energy and more brutality; then success would be assured. Not until the eighteenth century did men begin to understand that interventionism is necessarily doomed to fail. The classical economists demonstrated that each constellation of the market has a corresponding price structure. Prices, wages, and interest rates are the result of the interplay of demand and supply. There are forces operating in the market which tend to restore this—natural—state if it is disturbed. Government decrees, instead of achieving the particular ends they seek, tend only to derange the working of the market and imperil the satisfaction of the needs of the consumers.

[Etatism and Autarky, pages 72–73] Interventionism aims at state control of market conditions. As the sovereignty of the national state is limited to the territory subject to its supremacy and has no jurisdiction outside its boundaries, it considers all kinds of international economic relations as serious obstacles to its policy. The ultimate goal of its foreign trade policy is economic self-sufficiency.

The avowed tendency of this policy is, of course, only to reduce imports as far as possible; but as exports have no purpose but to pay for imports, they drop concomitantly. . . .

The essential goal of socialist production, according to Marx, is the elimination of the market. As long as a socialist community is still forced to sell a part of its production abroad—whether to foreign socialist governments or to foreign business—it still produces for a market and is subject to the laws of the market economy. A socialist system is defective as such as long as it is not economically self-sufficient.

The international division of labor is a more efficient system of production than is the economic autarky of every nation. The same amount of labor and of material factors of production yields a higher output. This surplus production benefits everyone concerned. Protectionism and autarky always result in shifting production from the centers where conditions are more favorable—i.e., from where the output for the same amount of physical input is higher—to the centers where they are less favorable. The more productive resources remain unused while the less productive are utilized. The effect is a general drop in the productivity of human effort, and thereby a lowering of the standard of living all over the world.

APPENDIX (1978): Interventionism

For readers who have not read other books of Mises which define terms he uses, the following is his definition of Interventionism in *Omnipotent Government*, Yale University Press, New Haven, Connecticut, 1944, page 59:

> In defiance of economic science the very popular doctrine of modern interventionism asserts that there is a system of economic cooperation, feasible as a permanent form of economic organization, which is neither capitalism nor socialism. This third system is conceived as an order based on private ownership of the means of production in which, however, the government intervenes, by orders and prohibitions, in the exercise of ownership rights. It is claimed that this system of interventionism is as far from socialism as it is from capitalism; that it offers a third solution of the problem of social organization; that it stands midway between socialism and capitalism; and that while retaining the advantages of both it escapes the disadvantages inherent in each of them. Such are the pretensions of interventionism as advocated by the older German school of étatism, by the American Institutionalists, and by many groups in other countries. Interventionism is practiced—except for socialist countries like Russia and Nazi Germany—by every contemporary government. The outstanding examples of interventionist policies are the *Sozialpolitik* of imperial Germany and the New Deal policy of present-day America.

III

The Austrian Problem

The polyglot state of the Habsburgs could have served a grand purpose. It could have provided a constitution that enabled peoples with different languages to live together harmoniously in one state. The Constitution of 1867, designed by Perthaler, sought to achieve just that. But the attempt was destined to fail because the grandees of the Sudetenland — the party in power — fought liberalism with all means at their disposal.

Thus Austria* around 1900 was a state unwanted by its subjects. The nationality† principle denied to Austria-Hungary its justification for existence, and everyone expected its early dissolution.

Only in Vienna there were still some people who were concerned about the preservation of the state. The events triggered by the dissolution of the Habsburg monarchy eventually revealed that these men endeavored to save Europe and civilization from a great catastrophe. But their efforts had to be in vain, because they lacked a viable ideological foundation.

This lack was clearly visible in the fact that no one was willing to concede sincerity to those men who had the future of Austria at heart. One could be a "good" (that is, nationalistic) German, Czech, Pole, etc. As a German cleric or Bohemian grandee one could be colorless nationally [in respect to language], and might care only about the interests of one's region or class. But to think more broadly as an "Austrian," that was considered to be the characteristic of a man who sought favors from the Crown. However, this was not really true. The "Crown" did not favor such strong loyalists; it favored the "moderate" irredentists.[1]

---

* Austria and Habsburg in this chapter refer to the Austro-Hungarian empire.
† In this chapter the term "national" refers generally to a linguistic or a sub-political group, and the term is in contrast to Austria-Hungary as a unity.
1. Irredentists are those who advocate the reincorporation of lands that are linguistically, culturally, and historically considered a part of their nation.

No one in Vienna could avoid pondering about national problems. In the *Socialwissenschaftlicher Bildungsverein* (Association for Education in the Social Sciences) Otto Bauer and Karl Renner presented their ideas, later published in their books, that served to promote a program of national autonomy. Ludo Hartmann reported on his investigations into the problems of linguistic assimilation, which unfortunately were never published. Adolf Bernatzik, professor of public law at the University, drew my attention to the problem of "national voting registration" that was to provide the basis for uniform election standards.

I watched all these efforts with great interest, but had my doubts about their success. It could not be denied that the people of the Danube Monarchy [Austria-Hungary] wished to destroy that entity. And, indeed, the question arose whether a state that was ruled by frivolous uneducated counts and ambitious unprincipled officials, was worth defending. The events that led to the downfall of the Körber administration made a deep impression on all those who were concerned about the preservation of the state. Among the many prime ministers who governed old Austria during the last twenty-five years [before 1914], Ernest von Körber was the only one who conducted a policy of state preservation. In this he was supported by the highly intelligent Rudolf Sieghart, his senior member of the cabinet. [Eugen von] Böhm-Bawerk served in that cabinet as Minister of Finance. Herr Körber had instructed his district attorneys to adopt a more tolerant policy toward closing down newspapers. Thus it happened that, when a German-nationalistic paper in Vienna published an article reviling the altar sacrament, that article had not been challenged. Körber's foes seized upon this omission as an opportunity to topple the Körber administration. Father confessors and ladies at the courts of the archduchesses worked diligently to pillory as sacrilegious the "Jew" Körber (one of his grandmothers or great-grandmothers had been Jewish). Thus the last chief executive who was sincerely concerned about the continuation of the state was removed from office.

I readily admit now that I—at that time—judged the shortcomings of Austrian affairs too severely, and that foreign conditions which I knew only from books or short superficial visits appeared to me in too favorable a light. But this did not alter the facts. The Habsburg state, which did not have the support of the ideological foundation of the nationality [unity of language] principle, could not endure the degree of political mismanagement that was common abroad. Mistakes that could be borne by national [single-language] states could be fatal to Austria. Harmful policy would destroy it more readily than it would destroy the English or French states.

The fact that state [political] and national [linguistic] lines did not coincide in Austria induced us to study problems which in states having language unity could easily be neglected. The English and French languages are still lacking the terms that permit a correct presentation of the political and economic problems that sprang from this Austrian type of dualism.

I interested myself particularly in what the special consequences of state interventionism would be specifically in the Austro-Hungarian empire. Every single interventionist measure must disturb the several individual national interests and strengths. The Austrian politicians knew this very well, and the reports of the Council of the Reich, of the provincial diets, and of the press contained abundant material about it. But the full extent of these problems became known to me only when, in 1909, I joined the Viennese Chamber of Commerce and became a member of the Central Committee on Trade Policy.

I intended to study these problems in great detail. When I conducted my first University seminar during the academic year 1913–1914, I chose four young doctors for research into the position of the Germans, Czechs, Poles, and Hungarians regarding foreign trade policy of the Austro-Hungarian customs union. They were to study especially those measures by which the Hungarian government and the autonomous provincial governments sought within the customs union to create administrative protection in favor of their [particular] nationals [in their several language groups]. I hoped to find yet a fifth collaborator for research on Italian questions. I planned myself to write a comprehensive report which was to be published together with the work of my colleagues.

Of these four young scholars, two were killed during the early weeks of the war. The third became "missing in action" during the fighting in the Carpathian Mountains in the winter of 1914–1915. The fourth was captured by the Russians in Wolhynia, in July 1916; we never heard from him or about him again.

IV

The Austrian School of Economics

When I first arrived at the University, Carl Menger was close to the termination of his teaching career. The idea that there was an Austrian School of economics was itself hardly recognized at the University, and I myself was not at all interested in it at that time.

Around Christmas, 1903, I read Menger's *Grundsätze der Volkswirtschaftslehre* for the first time.[1] It was the reading of this book that made an "economist" of me.

Personally I met Carl Menger only many years later. He was then already more than seventy years old, hard of hearing, and plagued by an eye disorder. But his mind was young and vigorous. Again and again I have asked myself why this man did not make better use of the last decades of his life. The fact that he still could do brilliant work if he wanted to do so was shown by his essay, *"Geld"* ("Money"), which he contributed to the *Handwörterbuch der Staatswissenschaften* (*Encyclopedia of State Sciences*).

I believe I know what discouraged Menger and what silenced him so early. His sharp mind had recognized the destiny of Austria, of Europe, and of the world. He saw the greatest and most advanced of all civilizations [nineteenth and twentieth century Western Europe] rushing to the abyss of destruction. He foresaw all the horrors which we are experiencing today [1940, World War II]. He knew the consequences of the world's turning away from true Liberalism [not the contrary Leftist so-called liberalism in the United States] and Capitalism. Nonetheless, he did what he could do to stem the tide. His book *Untersuchungen über die Methode der Socialwissenschaften und der Politischen Oekonomie insbesondere* was meant as a polemic essay

---

1. German publication, 1872; English translation, *Principles of Economics* (Free Press of Glencoe, 1950).

against all those pernicious intellectual currents that were poisoning the world from the universities of "Great Prussia."[2] The knowledge that his fight was without expectation of success, however, sapped his strength. He had transmitted this pessimism to his young student and friend, Archduke Rudolf, successor to the Austro-Hungarian throne. The Archduke committed suicide because he despaired about the future of his empire and the fate of European civilization, not because of a woman. (He took a young girl along in death who, too, wished to die; but he did not commit suicide on her account.)

My grandfather [on my mother's side] had a brother who died several years before I was born. The brother, Dr. Joachim Landau, had been a liberal deputy in the Austrian Parliament and a close friend of his party colleague, deputy Dr. Max Menger, a brother of Carl Menger. One day Joachim Landau told my grandfather about a conversation he had had with Carl Menger.

According to my grandfather, as told to me around 1910, Carl Menger had made the following remarks: "The policies as conducted by the European powers will lead to a horrible war that will end with gruesome revolutions, with the extinction of European culture and the destruction of prosperity of all nations. In preparation for these inevitable events investments only in gold hoards, and perhaps in obligations of the two Scandinavian countries can be recommended." In fact, Menger had his savings invested in Swedish obligations. Whoever foresees so clearly before the age of forty the disaster and the destruction of everything he deems of value, cannot escape pessimism and psychic depression. What kind of a life would King Priam have had, the old rhetors were accustomed to ask, if at the age of twenty he already would have foreseen the fall of ancient Troy! Carl Menger had barely half of his life behind him when he foresaw the inevitability of the fall of his Troy.

The same pessimism overshadowed other sharp-sighted Austrians. Being Austrian afforded the sad privilege of having a better opportunity to recognize fate and destiny. Grillparzer's melancholy and peevishness arose from this source. The feeling of facing powerlessly the coming evil drove the most able and noble of all Austrian patriots, Adolf Fischhof, into loneliness.

---

2. German publication, 1883; English translation (University of Illinois Press, 1963); *Investigations into the Method of the Social Sciences with Special Reference to Economics* (NYU Press, 1985).

For obvious reasons I frequently discussed Knapp's *Staatliche Theorie des Geldes* with Menger.[3] His answer was, "It is the logical development of Prussian police science. What are we to think of a nation whose elite, after two hundred years of economics, admire such nonsense, which is not even new, as highest revelation? What can we still expect of such a nation?"

Menger's successor at the University was Friedrich von Wieser. He was a highly cultured gentleman, had a fine intellect, and was an honest scholar. Before many others, he was fortunate to become acquainted with the work of Menger, the significance of which he recognized immediately. He enriched the thought in some respects, although he was no creative thinker and in general was more harmful than useful. He never really understood the gist of the idea of Subjectivism in the Austrian School of thought, which limitation caused him to make many unfortunate mistakes. His imputation theory is untenable. His ideas on value calculation justify the conclusion that he could not be called a member of the Austrian School, but rather was a member of the Lausanne School [Leon Walras et al. and the idea of economic equilibrium], which in Austria was represented brilliantly by Rudolf Auspitz and Richard Lieben.

What distinguishes the Austrian School and will lend it immortal fame is precisely the fact that it created a theory of economic action and not of economic equilibrium or non-action. The Austrian School, too, uses the idea of rest and equilibrium, which economic thought cannot do without. But it is always aware of the purely instrumental nature of such an idea, and similar aids. The Austrian School endeavors to explain prices that are really paid in the market, and not just prices that would be paid under certain, never realizable conditions. It rejects the mathematical method, not because of ignorance of mathematics or aversion to mathematical exactness, but because it does not emphasize a detailed description of a state of hypothetical static equilibrium. It has never suffered from the illusion that values can be measured. It has never misunderstood that statistical data belong to economic history only, and that statistics have nothing to do with economic theory.

Because Austrian economics is a theory of human action, [Josef

---

3. German publication, 1905; English translation, *The State Theory of Money*, 1924; Kelley and Millman, 1973.

Alois] Schumpeter does not belong to the Austrian School. In his first book he significantly related himself to Wieser and Walras, but not to Menger and Böhm-Bawerk. Economics, to him, is a theory of "economic quantities," and not of human action. Schumpeter's *Theory of Economic Development* is a typical product of the equilibrium theory.

At this point it may be necessary to correct a misunderstanding created by the term, "Austrian School of Economics." Neither Menger nor Böhm-Bawerk desired to found a "school" in the sense this term is customarily used in university circles. In their seminars the true Austrians never sought to make young students their blind disciples, and then to provide them with professorships. They knew that through books and economic instruction they could promote an understanding of economic problems and thus render important services to society. But they also knew that economists could not be reared. As pioneers and creative thinkers they were fully aware that scientific progress cannot be organized and innovation created, according to plan. They never attempted to propagandize their theories. Truth will prevail by its own force if man has the ability to perceive it. If he lacks this ability, it will be useless by dubious means to extract lip service from people who cannot comprehend the content and significance of a doctrine.

Carl Menger never tried to extend favors to his colleagues, who would then return such favors through recommendations for appointments. Böhm-Bawerk, at first as Minister of Finance and later as ex-minister, could have used his influence; but he always disparaged such behavior. Menger occasionally and without success tried to prevent the promotion of people who, like Zwiedineck, were unaware of what was going on in economics. Böhm-Bawerk did not even attempt that. He promoted rather than hindered the appointments of Professors Gottl and Spann to the Technical Institute at Brno.

Menger's position in this regard is best illustrated by a statement which [Friedrich A. von] Hayek found when going through Menger's scientific literary papers. It reads: "There is only one sure method for the final victory of a scientific idea, namely, by letting every contrary proposition run a free and full course" [in a sense, destroy itself]. Schmoller, Bücher, and Lujo Brentano practiced a different view. They deprived everyone, who did not blindly follow them, of the opportunity to teach at German universities.

Thus [by the absence of a policy of selecting personnel favoring Austrian ideology] the professorships at Austro-Hungarian universities fell into the hands of young representatives of Prussian historicism. Alfred Weber and Spiethoff in succession held a position at the University of Prague. A certain Professor Guenther became professor of economics in Innsbruck. I mention this only in order to put in its proper light Franz Oppenheimer's assertion that the marginal utility theory monopolized the teaching position in economics. For several years Schumpeter was full professor in Bonn. He was the only case in which a German university appointed a teacher who belonged to modern economics.[4] Among the many hundreds of men who between 1870 and 1934 taught economics at German universities, not a single professor was acquainted with the works of the Austrian or Lausanne Schools, or modern Anglo-Saxon economics. No unsalaried lecturer [*Privatdozent*, in the German university system] who was suspected of belonging to these schools was ever admitted to a faculty. Knies and Dietzel were the last economists at German universities. In the German Reich they did not teach economics, but Marxism or Nazism. The same was true at the universities of Czarist Russia where they taught "legalistic" Marxism or economic history, not economics. That, in contrast, in Austria a few professors and unsalaried lecturers were permitted to teach economics was an affront to the totality claim of the German "economic state sciences."

The Austrian School of Economics was peculiarly Austrian in the sense that it grew in the soil of an Austrian culture, which Nazism later crushed. In this soil Franz Brentano's philosophy could grow roots, as could Bolzano's epistemology, Mach's empiricism, Husserl's phenomenology, and Breuer's and Freud's psychoanalysis. In Austria the air was free from the specter of Hegelian dialectics. There was no mood, in the sense of a national duty, to "overcome" the ideas of Western Europe. In Austria, eudaemonism, hedonism, and utilitarianism were not scorned; they were studied.

It would be a mistake to believe that the Austrian government promoted all these great movements. On the contrary, it dismissed from teaching Bolzano and Brentano; it isolated Mach, and did not at all care for Husserl, Breuer, and Freud. It appreciated Böhm-Bawerk as a capable official; not as an economist.

Böhm-Bawerk had been professor in Innsbruck, but he soon tired

4. In Mises's view, "modern economics" was the subjective marginal utility economics of Menger and Böhm-Bawerk, which had clearly superseded the classical economics of Adam Smith and David Ricardo and Marx's labor theory of value.

of his position. The barren intellectual climate of this University, of the city, and of the province became unbearable to him. He preferred employment in the Ministry of Finance in Vienna. When he finally left government service, he was offered a sizeable pension which he rejected for a professorship at the University of Vienna.

When Böhm-Bawerk opened his seminar it was a great day in the history of the University and the development of economics. As the subject matter of the first seminar, Böhm-Bawerk chose the fundamentals of the theory of value. From his Marxian position, Otto Bauer sought to dissect the subjectivism of the Austrian value theory. With the other members of the seminar in the background, the discussion between Bauer and Böhm-Bawerk filled the whole winter semester. Bauer's brilliant intellect was very impressive; he was a worthy opponent of the great master whose critique had mortally wounded Marxian economics. I believe that in the end Bauer had to admit to himself also that the Marxian labor theory of value was untenable. Bauer abandoned his intention to write a reply to Böhm-Bawerk's critique of Marx.* The first volume of the Marx series contained a sensational rejoinder by Hilferding to Böhm-Bawerk. Bauer, however, admitted to me often that Hilferding had never really even comprehended the nature of the problem!

I attended Böhm-Bawerk's seminar regularly until I qualified for lecturing in 1913. During the last two winter semesters that I still attended the Böhm-Bawerk seminar, we discussed my *The Theory of Money and Credit*.[5] In the first semester we dealt with my explanation of the purchasing power of money, and during the second with my trade cycle theory. The difference of opinion that emerged between my position and that of Böhm-Bawerk will be dealt with later; see Chapter VI, page 38.

Böhm-Bawerk was a brilliant seminar leader. He did not think of himself as a teacher, but as a chairman who occasionally also participated in the discussion. Unfortunately, the extraordinary freedom to

* For Böhm-Bawerk's critique of Marx, see Volume I of the three-volume *Capital and Interest, History and Critique of Interest Theories*, pp. 281–306 (Libertarian Press, South Holland, Illinois, 1959). Or see the paperback extract from Volume I, *The Exploitation Theory of Socialism-Communism*, pp. 53–84 (LP, 1975). See also *Shorter Classics of Böhm-Bawerk*, Essay IV, "Unsolved Contradiction in the Marxian Economic System," pp. 201–302 (LP, 1962).
5. German editions, 1912, 1924; English translation, 1934; expanded (Yale, 1953; Liberty Fund, 1980).

speak which he granted to every member was occasionally abused by thoughtless talkers. Especially disturbing was the nonsense which Otto Neurath presented with fanatical fervor. Stronger use of the responsibilities inherent in a chairmanship would often have improved the situation, but Böhm-Bawerk wanted no part of it. In science he believed, as did Menger, that everyone should be permitted to speak.

The lifework of Böhm-Bawerk lies before us in splendid completion.[6] His masterly critique of the old economics and his own theory have enriched us forever. And yet, it must be stated that Böhm-Bawerk could have produced much more if conditions had permitted it. In his seminar presentations and in personal conversations he developed thoughts that extended far beyond those which are presented in his writings. But his physical constitution could no longer withstand the hard work necessary to embark upon great works—his nerves were failing him. The two-hour seminar already taxed his strength. Only through great regularity of life habits could he gather the strength needed for his scientific work in economics, to which his life belonged completely. Recreation and enjoyment he found in philharmonic concerts.

The evening of Böhm-Bawerk's life was darkened by his fears for the future of Austria and its culture. He died from a heart attack a few weeks after the outbreak of the war. I received the news one evening early in September 1914 when I was with my artillery battery at the front, east of Trampol. As I returned from a patrol ride I was handed a newspaper that carried a full obituary of Böhm-Bawerk.

6. Now in English translation by Hans F. Sennholz, *Capital and Interest*, 3 volumes (Libertarian Press, 1959).

V

First Writings on the Theory of Money

Karl Helfferich, in his book, *Das Geld*, published in 1903, asserted that the marginal utility theory of the Austrians had failed to solve the problem of money value. Therefore, I intended to investigate the validity of this charge and beginning in 1906 devoted a great deal of fervent effort to the problems of money and banking. I studied the great theoretical works as well as the history of currencies of the European countries, the United States, British India and, in general, sought to find my way through the wealth of literature. [This culminated in my writing three essays.]

1. As my first literary effort, I published an essay in Volume XVI of *Zeitschrift für Volkswirtschaft, Sozialpolitik und Verwaltung (Journal for Economics, Social Policy and Administration**), with the title, "*Die wirtschaftspolitischen Motive der österreichischen Valutaregulierung*" ("The Economic Motives of Austrian Foreign Exchange Controls").

2. In the fall of 1908 Professor Edgeworth [in England] asked Professor Philippovich [in Austria] to contribute an article to the *Economic Journal*. Such an essay, to be no longer than ten pages, was to analyze for the English-speaking world the foreign exchange policy of the Austro-Hungarian Central Bank. Philippovich declined and recommended me to be the author. I accepted.[1]

3. And I also decided to deal with the topic more extensively in the German language. This German essay, under the title, "*Das Problem gesetzlicher Aufnahme der Barzahlungen in Oesterreich-Ungarn*" ["The Problem of Legal Resumption of Gold Payments in Austria-Hungary"],

---

* Title translation only; not available in English edition.
1. Mises's English-language article was published as "The Foreign Exchange Policy of the Austro-Hungarian Bank" in *The Economic Journal*, June 1909, pp. 201–211.

which appeared in Schmoller's *Yearbook* in the spring of 1909, generated furious protest among the most powerful members of the Austrian inflation party.

During my research for the aforementioned three essays I gradually came to recognize the worst shortcomings of the prevailing monetary thought. I was convinced of the indefensibility of the balance-of-payments theory and of the doctrine of "elasticity" of bank credit; but brief essays on economic history and policy do not lend themselves to analyzing important questions definitively. I had to postpone this task for the theoretical work I planned to do later, and for the time being move within the generally accepted thought structure.

I am by-passing here my critique of Knapp's discussion of the foreign exchange policies of central banks. Knapp's doctrines, which were then generally admired in Germany and Eastern Europe, have long been forgotten. But anyone studying the decline of German thought in general and German economic thought in particular, will find the most remarkable and psychologically interesting material in those parts of Knapp's doctrine, which I criticized in the sixth section of my essay, "The Problem of Legal Resumption of Gold Payments in Austria-Hungary." For instance, Knapp spoke about losses the central bank suffered from foreign exchange policy and urged the state to reimburse it for these losses. But a mere cursory look at the bank's balance sheets and income statements should have revealed that the foreign exchange transactions yielded considerable profits, in which the state actually had participated.

My essay dealt with the problems of *de jure* resumption of gold redemption of the notes of the Austro-Hungarian Central Bank. For a number of years the Bank, without hesitation or discrimination, had *de facto* met all demands for foreign exchange at a rate that in no case exceeded the lawful gold parity of the crown by more than the margin, which in gold-standard countries is called the upper gold point. Thus Austria-Hungary had, in fact, resumed gold payments. Now it was under discussion whether this *de facto* situation should be made a legal obligation. One consideration that *favored* this change was the more favorable conditions under which foreign money markets would grant loans in Austrian crown denomination, if such gold payments for notes were no longer at the voluntary discretion of the Bank. Hungary especially raised this argument. The negative attitude of the Bank management and of some Austrian circles, according to Hungary, reflected the Bank's desire to perpetuate the Hungarian dependence on Viennese money markets, and render it impossible to tap the sources of cheaper money in other countries in Western Europe. There were no cogent reasons *against* the legalization of the condition that existed already in fact.

The opponents of legally requiring resumption of gold payments were advancing an indefensible theory in support of their position. A bank that is legally obligated to make gold payment, they argued, must adjust its discount rate to the conditions prevailing in the world markets. But the Austro-Hungarian Bank, they averred, was in a more favorable position because it was not legally obligated to redeem its notes. The Bank was in a position to differentiate between legitimate and illegitimate demand. Demand was said to be illegitimate if it aimed at shifting funds abroad in order to take advantage of higher interest rates abroad. The Bank should make it its policy never to meet this demand of interest rate arbitrage; it should only satisfy legitimate demand. It thus could avoid, or at least postpone, raising its rates, which required redemption that was legally obligatory.

This doctrine was completely erroneous. The Bank never made a distinction between legitimate and illegitimate demand; since 1900 it had met all demands for payment. But if it had followed the advice of the opponents of legalization, the arbitrage speculators would have sought to buy foreign exchange in the open market, which would have raised the exchange rate and depreciated the Austrian currency.

The doctrine was neither new nor specifically Austrian. It was the old fallacy that had been expounded fifteen and twenty years earlier about the advantages of the French gold premium policy. But the French advocates had not denied that such a policy would cause exchange rates to rise. They recommended the policy for France which then was one of the great capital exporting countries, and not for importing countries, such as Austria-Hungary. For a debtor country to relax its ties with foreign money markets would raise the cost of its credits, not reduce it.

I had just completed my essay when an invitation by the Vice President of the [Austrian Central] Bank surprised me. During my visit with him in his office, Herr Waldmayer told me that he had heard from Professor Landesberger that I needed material for a study of Bank policy and that he would be delighted to make it available to me. He further added that I would then be required to submit my work to the

Bank management before it could go to press. I declined politely but firmly. I did not then know Professor Landesberger, but knew that he was a good friend of Professor Philippovich. I suspected that Philippovich had shown Landesberger my essay or told Landesberger of its content.

I gained the impression from my conversation with Herr Waldmayer that the Bank management was greatly interested in continuing the existing conditions. I could not understand this. Indeed, I knew that a legal requirement of gold payment would curtail the Bank's right to invest some reserves in foreign accounts and obligations yielding an interest, and that this would reduce the Bank's gross returns. This would above all hurt the Bank's stockholders and both states [Austria and Hungary] sharing in the Bank's returns. Through changes in the tax laws the Secretaries of both Treasuries would probably have seen to it that this loss would fall completely or mainly on the stockholders; no one represented their interests, least of all the Bank management which had been appointed jointly by the two governments. When I left Herr Waldmayer's office I had the impression that he would have offered me a sizeable sum if only I had been a little less recalcitrant. The Bank disposed officially over certain press funds for such purposes.

An explanation came to me a few years later when, in 1912, I published an article on the fourth renewal of the Bank's privileges, and was again attacked by the opponents of gold payment. At that time Böhm-Bawerk, who was Secretary of the Treasury, informed me of the reasons for the Bank's opposition to my ideas on this subject. According to Böhm-Bawerk, a part of the proceeds from the obligations invested abroad was credited to a special and secret account, which was at the sole discretion of the Bank's governor. Highly paid Bank officials, government officials who supervised the Bank, journalists, politicians, and occasionally also other men, received considerable sums from this confidential fund. He, Böhm-Bawerk, had learned of its existence only by chance, when the Hungarian Secretary of the Treasury complained that the share paid to Austrians was too large in comparison with that paid to Hungarians. The whole affair displeased Böhm-Bawerk greatly, and gave him a distaste for his position or for any service in the administration. The Hungarian Secretary, however, opposed Böhm-Bawerk's intention to abolish the fund. But, so Böhm-Bawerk concluded, "I consider it my obligation to inform you so that you may understand the background for the attacks on you." I had to promise him not to reveal the affair unless I heard about it from other sources. In fact, I have been silent until today, although a few years after the war the former press secretary of the Bank on his own volition told me about the use of the fund. The sums in this case were more modest than those of Bismarck's famous *Reptilienfonds** (Reptile Fund) but they sufficed to explain the strong opposition of the Bank management and other men against a reform which could have dried up this source.

The strongest attack against my arguments came from Walter Federn, the publisher of an economics journal, *Oesterreichischer Volkswirt* [*The Austrian Economist*]. Federn had held small positions in banks and then had become stock exchange reporter for several newspapers. For several years he had been publishing *The Austrian Economist* which was financed by a friend of his, bank director Rosenbaum. Federn was ignorant in economics, and had read almost no books on economics except Knapp's *State Theory of Money*. He had limited knowledge of economic conditions and statistics, was completely uncritical, and was unable to think independently. In general he was thought of as an intellectual duffer, although his fluent style of writing was generally praised. In addition to Rosenbaum's subsidies, the main revenue source of his journal, which then had only a few subscribers, were the cash "contributions" which banks and large corporations paid newspapers and weekly and monthly economic journals for carrying advertising, balance sheets and income statements, and announcements of stockholder meetings. No special conditions were attached

---

* The *Encyclopaedia Britannica* reports on the Guelph Fund later called *Reptilienfonds*: "The main tasks that lay before the German government after 1870 were the assimilation of the administration and the economic development of the country. On the whole, the provinces accepted their fate with equanimity, though in Hanover especially the deposed dynasty continued to command a considerable following. Since the dispossessed princes refused to resign their claims, the large sum of money which had been assigned to them by the Prussian parliament was, as early as March 1868, sequestrated and under the name of the Guelph Fund (*Welfenfonds*) formed a secret service supply highly convenient for Bismarck's purposes."

The government used these funds partly for useful purposes in the Hanover province; they constructed dams, dikes, barracks, built theaters, museums, picture galleries. But besides these occasional useful applications, Bismarck used the money chiefly for political purposes, especially for founding newspapers or helping existing ones. People called not only these papers "reptiles," but also the people who secretly worked for these papers. In the course of time there was not one city in the country where there were no "reptiles." Even in foreign countries one or the other paper had connections with the *Reptilienfonds* and thus the money was gradually spent for the printing presses, with buying off uncomfortable correspondents and silencing others.

[Excerpts from the German *Geschichte des deutschen Liberalismus*, Oskar Klein-Hattingen (Berlin-Schoneberg: Fortschritt, 1912). Collected by MvM.]

to these contributions. It is true, the newspaper publishers feared interruption of further contributions in retaliation against an especially ugly attack by the magazine on a corporate subscriber; but it was permissible to publish moderate critiques of an enterprise that made such contributions.

It was not these contributions that deprived Viennese journalists of their independence; it was their ignorance that fettered them; the great age of Viennese economic journalism had long passed away. The excellent economists who had collaborated with the press—among them Carl Menger—had found no worthy successors. Only the editorial staff of the *Neue Freie Presse* (*New Free Press*) and *Neues Wiener Tagblatt* (*New Viennese Daily*) still had economists with knowledge and intelligence. All other editors were ignorant and dull; they depended on information from interested parties. Stock exchange reporters received their information from the stock exchange men who in such matters were spokesmen of the big banks. When a government regulation was passed or an important business transaction took place, the journalists would rush to the pertinent government official or to the businessman concerned. The information the journalists received from him was then presented to the public. The government did not need to corrupt journalists; it was enough to inform them. Journalists feared nothing more than their being informed a few days later than others in their profession. To avoid such a penalty they were always prepared to represent the government's point of view. Their economic ignorance then afforded the advantage that they could plead the government case without independent mental reservations.

Some two years before the publication of my essay Herr Federn had been initiated into the problems of foreign exchange by the Bank officials. In several articles in Viennese newspapers and in the *Frankfurter Zeitung* he had published what he had learned from them. He was very proud of this work, which he thought to be a great journalistic achievement; and my critique of the Bank's policy hurt his vanity, which was what primarily explains the fanatical fervor of his attacks. Of course, his desire to please the Bank officials and the Treasury also played a role. But Federn did not take the Bank's position because he was receiving secret payments from it. I am convinced that he was unaware that any such subsidies came from an irregular secret fund, which a legalization of gold payment would have jeopardized. Individuals could receive Bank money in good faith as the Bank was also using funds that were derived from open revenues. Those who did not know the total amount spent on the press and other protected favorites could assume that the endowment of the press fund was legal.

When Böhm-Bawerk revealed to me the secret of the Bank's special disposition fund, I was faced with a new problem. I had then been established for several years. For several months I had worked in the Treasury and the public prosecutor's office, and for two years with the court, and since 1909 I had been with the Chamber of Commerce. I recognized the corruption that is an inescapable symptom of interventionism, and knew very well that it extended to the highest posts of the state. But this was the first time that in a scientific exchange I met opponents whose motives were not objective. What was I to do? After long and thorough consideration I finally arrived at a clear position.

An economist must deal with doctrines, not with men. He must criticize erroneous thought. It is not his function to reveal personal motives for protecting fallacies. An economist must face his opponents with the fictitious assumption that they are guided by objective considerations only. It is irrelevant whether the advocate of a fallacious opinion acts in good or bad faith; it matters only whether the stated opinion is correct or fallacious. It is the task of other people to reveal corruption and inform the public about it.

Throughout my life I have held to these principles. I knew a great deal, if not all, about the corruption of interventionists and socialists with which I had to cope. But I never made use of this knowledge, which was not always properly understood by others. As the Viennese Social Democrats [Socialists] always attacked me in an ugly manner, people supplied me with massive material on the corrupt practices of socialist leaders. Even without the help of these informers I was well aware of the moral decadence within the party. I would not have needed the material that was offered if I had wanted to deal in such disclosures. It was often held against me that I politely rejected offers to supply me with proof, admissible in courts of law, of embezzlements and frauds by my opponents.

During the crises created by the Balkan War, in the winter of 1912–1913, the Austro-Hungarian Bank really tried not to meet a part of the demand for foreign exchange. Naturally the consequence was a greater demand on the open market and a rise in foreign exchange rates. The Bank immediately had to return to its old policy of unlimited and unconditional sale of foreign exchange. It considered itself exceptionally smart in slightly increasing the rate at which it was willing to sell. But it merely achieved thereby a decline in confidence in the Austrian currency, and a withdrawal of considerable sums of foreign short-term money invested in Austria.

It was the express goal of inflationists to reduce the purchasing power of the Austrian crown relative to gold, foreign exchange, and international economic goods. This was readily admitted by the intelligent opponents of gold payment, such as Professor Landesberger and the chairman of the tariff division of the Department of Commerce, Richard Riedl. Only a noninformed man such as Federn could believe that a refusal of note redemption would not affect the stability of exchange rates. The inflationists welcomed a small devaluation of the crown as a first step on a road they approved. They only regretted that the Bank immediately returned to a policy of unconditional redemption in gold. That they blamed me for this return was not without reason.

Naturally I was fully aware that public opinion in Austria was in favor of inflationism, and that besides me there were only a few others who supported a policy of stable exchange rates. The Minister of Finance at that time was a Pole, Count Zaleski, who, before his purely political appointment, had never dealt with financial problems. He readily admitted his ignorance in the financial field. In a conversation that took place in the home of a mutual friend, Count Zaleski explained to me: "I was told by members of the Polish Club (of the House of Deputies) that a rise in foreign exchange rates must be seen as a favorable phenomenon rather than an unfavorable one. For agriculture, a ten percent rise would be a direct blessing."

This "blessing" was soon to come in plenteous measure!

VI

The Theory of Money and Credit

Upon completion of my two essays on the Bank's foreign exchange policy I intended to embark upon the development of my theory of money and credit. I barely had written the first pages when, in early January 1909, I was suddenly called to an unusual active duty. The so-called "Annexation Crisis" had induced the government to take special steps and hasten the modernization of the artillery.[1] I returned to Vienna in February, and on April 1 joined the Viennese Chamber of Commerce. And again, during the early months of my new activity, I found no time for my scientific work. I finally was able to begin in the fall. The finished manuscript was in the hands of the publisher early in 1912.

The greatest difficulty I faced in the preparation of the book was the fact that I meant to give attention to merely a limited part of the total scope of economic problems. But economics necessarily must be a complete and united whole. In economics there can be no specialization. To deal with a part one must do so on the foundation of a theory that comprises all the problems. But I could not use any of the existing comprehensive theories. The systems of Menger and Böhm-Bawerk were no longer wholly satisfactory to me. I was ready to proceed further on the road these old masters had discovered. But I could not use their treatment of those problems with which monetary theory must begin.

According to prevailing opinion at that time, the theory of money could be clearly separated from the total structure of economic prob-

A chronological list of the various editions of Ludwig von Mises's *The Theory of Money and Credit* appears at the end of this chapter.

1. For years, the Christians and Turks had been in conflict in the Balkans. Austria-Hungary had been authorized by treaty (1878) to occupy the area; the Austro-Hungarian government's decision to do so became known as the "Annexation Crisis."

lems—it did not, in fact, even belong with economics; in a certain
respect it was an independent discipline. In accordance with this opinion the universities in Anglo-Saxon countries had created special professorships for currency and banking. It was my intention to reveal this
position as erroneous and restore the theory of money to its appropriate
position as an integral part of the science of economics.

If I could have worked quietly and taken my time, I would have
begun with a theory of direct exchange in the first volume; and then
I could proceed to the theory of indirect exchange. But I actually began
with indirect exchange, because I believed that I did not have much
time; I knew that we were on the eve of a great war and I wanted to
complete my book before the war's outbreak. I thus decided that in a
few points only I would go beyond the narrow field of strictly monetary
theory, and would postpone my preparation of a more complete work.
I think I succeeded in my given task.

I must add expressly that my critique of Menger and Böhm-Bawerk
concerns less that which they have said than that which they left un-
said. I regretted that they had not replaced John Stuart Mill's unsatisfactory delineation of the field of economics with a more satisfactory
one. I found fault also because they had failed to criticize severely the
impermissible use of mathematical economics, and because they had
failed to elaborate more clearly their own point of view. I found especially that Böhm-Bawerk, in his discussion with Wieser, had failed
to touch upon many topics that were of decisive importance.

One point which I could not silently ignore, although it belongs to
the general value theory, was the problem of assumed measurement
of value, and the related problem of total value. In order to develop
the theory of money I had to refute the notion that there was such a
thing as (1) value calculation or even measurement; (2) that the "value"
of a total supply could be calculated from the known "value" of a part;
or (3) inversely that the "value" of any part could be obtained from the
known "value" of a total. I had to explode the hypostasis of "value" and
to demonstrate that there is an activity of valuing and acts of valuation,
but that the term "value" is permissible only when limited to denoting
an individually valued object, or to designate the result of a valuation
process.

I endeavored to cope with this task in the first chapters of my book
and especially to refute the fallacies of Irving Fisher and Schumpeter.
Toward this end Čuhel's book was very useful to me. Its author has

been forgotten today [1940]—his book is outdated; but there cannot be any doubt that in the end Čuhel will occupy a deservedly honored place in the history of our science.

The theory of determination and changes of the purchasing power of money takes as a starting point Menger's theory of cash holding. Everything that follows I had to create anew. As it is not my intention here to present an excerpt of my book, I merely would like to remark on the method I used and on its significance.

On all its pages I used the "step-by-step" method which is allegedly being rediscovered today [1940] as "period analysis" or "process analysis." It is the only permissible method, which renders superfluous the argument between short-run and long-run economics. It also makes the distinction between statics and dynamics an idle question. If no condition is considered "normal," if we are aware that the concept of a "static equilibrium" is alien to life and action which we study, and that this concept is merely a mental picture we use in order to comprehend abstractly human action through the idea of a state of non-action, then we must recognize that we always study motion, but never a state of equilibrium. All of mathematical economics with its beautiful equations and curves is nothing but useless doodling. The equations and curves must be preceded by non-mathematical considerations; setting up equations does not enhance our knowledge. Because there are no constant relations in the field of human action, the equations of mathematical catallactics cannot be made to serve practical problems in the same way the equations of mechanics solve practical problems through the use of data and constants that have been ascertained empirically.

In my book on money I did not say one controversial word against the mathematical school. I presented the correct doctrine and refrained from attacking the method of mathematicians. In fact, I even resisted the temptation to dissect the empty term "velocity." I refuted mathematical economics by proving that the quantity of money and the purchasing power of the monetary unit are not inversely proportional. This proof demonstrated that the only constant relationship which was believed to exist between "economic quantities" is a variable determined by the data of each individual case. It thus exploded the equations of exchange of Irving Fisher and Gustav Cassel.

The step-by-step analysis must consider the lapse of time. In such an analysis the time-lag between cause and effect becomes a multitude of time differences between single successive consequences. Reflection on these time-lags then leads to a precise theory of the social consequences of changes in the purchasing power of money.

Let me now remark on Böhm-Bawerk's reaction to my theory in order to explain more precisely my objections to the doctrines of both old masters, Menger and Böhm-Bawerk. And let me demonstrate with a concrete example the difference between the older and younger Austrian Schools. Both Menger and Böhm-Bawerk tacitly assumed the neutrality of money. They had developed the theory of direct exchange and held to the opinion that all problems of economic theory could be solved with the imaginary concept of market exchanges without the use of money. My theory of the inevitable non-neutrality of money now made this position untenable. But Böhm-Bawerk refused to admit this. He raised no objections against the cogency of my step-by-step analysis; he did not deny its results—namely, that changes in purchasing power of money cause prices of different commodities and services to change neither simultaneously nor evenly, and that it is incorrect to maintain that changes in the quantity of money bring about simultaneous and proportional changes in the "level" of prices. But he maintained that this was a "friction phenomenon." According to him, the old doctrine was correct "in principle" and maintains its full significance for an analysis aimed at "purely economic action." In real life there is resistance and friction which cause the result to deviate from that arrived at theoretically. I tried in vain to convince Böhm-Bawerk of the inadmissibility of the use of metaphors borrowed from mechanics. As can be seen from his twofold organization of the tasks of the price theory, Böhm-Bawerk labored under the influence of Mill's interpretation.* I could have convinced him only if I, myself, had been clear about the basic problems. But I was still too much under the influence of Mill. Only many years later could I have refuted Böhm-Bawerk's doctrine of "direct exchange advantage."† My essay which deals with the teachings of Menger and Böhm-Bawerk was intended to be a worthy memorial to the two masters.[2]

---

* Author's Note: Cf. Böhm-Bawerk, *Capital and Interest*, Volume II, *Positive Theory of Capital*, pages 207–214, especially page 212 (South Holland, Illinois: Libertarian Press, 1959).

† Author's Note: Cf. my *Grundprobleme der Nationalökonomie*, Jena, 1933. English edition, *Epistemological Problems of Economics*, translated by George Reisman, D. Van Nostrand, Princeton, New Jersey, 1960, page 167 *et seq.*

2. See Mises's essay, "Remarks on the Fundamental Problem of the Subjective Theory of Value," first published, 1928; reprinted as chapter 5 in *Grundprobleme der Nationalökonomie.*

In the chapter on the determination of exchange ratios between different kinds of money I endeavored to restate Ricardo's irrefutable theory which the "balance-of-payment theory" has tried to replace. Gustav Cassel who soon thereafter presented Ricardo's theory in inappropriate form gave it the name of "purchasing power parity theory." During the 1920s it was called Cassel's theory if one agreed; and Mises's theory, if one disagreed. I repeat, it is Ricardo's theory, and neither Cassel's nor mine.

The second great problem I dealt with in my book was that of fiduciary media. I had to create this concept in order to overcome the prevailing confusion surrounding the term "credit." If no distinction is drawn between "commodity credit" (*Sachkredit*) and "fiduciary credit" (*Zirkulationskredit*), useful results can never be attained. Fritz Machlup very capably translated the two distinct concepts with the terms, "transfer credit" and "created credit." Only by the making of this distinction can the basis for a correct critique of the doctrine of "elasticity" of bank media of payment be developed, and can the way be paved for understanding how the creation of fiduciary credit explains business cycle phenomena. I am honored that it was named the Austrian Trade Cycle Theory.

In the last part of my book I endeavored to discuss currency and banking problems that were then of general interest. I concluded with the remark that the prevailing banking opinion would soon lead to catastrophic events.

As could be expected, my book was rejected summarily by the journals of the German social sciences. I paid little attention to that. I was convinced that my explanations would soon prevail. With dismay I observed the political and military catastrophe which I had forecast standing at the door.

New books, despite being appraised as "destroyed" by the critics, can be valuable and long-lived. Anyone who says only that which everyone wants to hear, had better remain silent. Men such as Knapp, Bendixen, Liefmann, Diehl, Adolf Wagner, and Bortkiewicz who then were celebrated in Germany as "monetary theorists" are no longer considered authorities.

The economist who first commended my work was Benjamin M. Anderson in his book, *The Value of Money*, published in 1917. I did not see his book until two years later (naturally, of course, because Austria was at war with the United States).

John Maynard Keynes reviewed my book in the first issue of the

Economic Journal that appeared after the outbreak of the war.* He gave it some praise: "the book is not to be denied considerable merit, . . . the book is 'enlightened in the highest degree' possible." But in general Keynes was greatly disappointed.

To him the book was "not constructive" and "not original"; there is "no lift in the book." And he added: "One closes the book, therefore, with a feeling of disappointment, that an author so intelligent, so candid and so widely read should, after all, help one so little to a clear understanding of the fundamentals of the subject." Sixteen years later Keynes admitted that his knowledge of the German language was rather poor. "In German," he wrote, "I can only clearly understand what I already know—so that new ideas are apt to be veiled from me by the difficulties of the language."†

It was not my fault that Keynes found my book neither original nor constructive, and that it could not guide him to a clear understanding of the problems.

APPENDIX (1978): Editions of *The Theory of Money and Credit*

The following is a chronological list of the various editions of *The Theory of Money and Credit* by Ludwig von Mises:

1912   First edition published in German: *Theorie des Geldes und der Umlaufsmittel.* München and Leipzig: Duncker & Humblot, 1912. xi:476 SS.

1924   Second edition published in German: *Theorie des Geldes und der Unlaufsmittel.* Revised. München and Leipzig: Duncker & Humblot, 1924. xv:420 SS.

1934   English translation of the second (1924) German edition: *The Theory of Money and Credit.* Translated by H. E. Batson. Introduction by Lionel Robbins. London: Jonathan Cape, 1934. 445 pp. index.

1936   Spanish translation of the second (1924) German edition: *Teoría del Dinero y del Crédito.* Translated by Antonio Riaño. Madrid: M. Aguilar, 1936. 490 pp.

---

* *Author's Note:* Cf. *Economic Journal*, Volume XXIV, pages 417–419.
† *Author's Note:* Cf. Keynes, *A Treatise on Money*, London, 1930, Volume I, page 199, note 2.

1949 Japanese translation of the second (1924) German edition: *Kahei oyobi Ryūtsū-Shudan no Riron*. Translated by Yoneo Azuma. Tokyo: Jitsūgyo no Nipponsha, 1949.

1953 Reprint of the English language translation (1934) of the second (German) edition, enlarged: *The Theory of Money and Credit*. Translated by H. E. Batson. New edition, enlarged with an essay on "Monetary Reconstruction." New Haven: Yale University Press, 1953. 493 pp. index.

1961 Spanish translation of the English language edition, enlarged (1953): *Teoría del Dinero y Crédito*. Translated by José Ma. Clarmunda Bes. Barcelona: Ediciones Zeus, 1961. 546 pp.

1961 Spanish translation of the 1953 essay, "Monetary Reconstruction," was printed as a separate booklet: *Reconstrucción Monetaria*. Translated by Gustavo R. Velasco. Buenos Aires: Centro de Estudios sobre la Libertad, 1961. 91 pp.

1969 Chinese translation by H. P. Yang. Taiwan (Republic of China): Taiwan Bank, Economic Research Department, 1969. 403 pp.

1971 Reprint of the English language (1953) edition: *The Theory of Money and Credit*. New edition, enlarged with an essay on "Monetary Reconstruction." Translated from the German by H. E. Batson. Irvington-on-Hudson, New York: The Foundation for Economic Education, Inc., 1971. 493 pp. index.

VII

First World War

I need not here report on the war, or my personal experiences during the war. This work is not concerned with military questions, nor does it deal with political matters any more than is absolutely necessary.

The war came as a result of an ideology that for hundreds of years had been proclaimed by all German institutions of learning. The professors of economics had contributed diligently to the intellectual preparation for war. They did not need to be re-trained in order to be converted into men of courage as the "intellectual bodyguard of the Hohenzollern." Schmoller authored the famous "Manifesto of 93" (October 11, 1914); another department chairman, Professor Schumacher, who later succeeded Schmoller in Berlin, edited the annexation program of the six central associations. Sombart wrote *Händler und Helden* (*Merchants and Heroes*).* Franz Oppenheimer would not be outdone in bewailing the French and English lack of culture. No longer did they teach economics; they were preaching the doctrines of war.

It was not much better in the enemy camp. But there were many who preferred to keep silent. For Edwin Cannan, however, it was the duty of economists to protest.

During the first fifteen months of the war, I could rarely find time to read a newspaper. Later conditions improved a little, and by the end of 1917 I was no longer at the front, but worked in the economics division of the Department of War. In those years I wrote only two small essays. The one on the classification of monetary theories was later added to the second edition [1924] of *The Theory of Money and Credit*. The other on *"Vom Ziel der Handelspolitik"* ("The Objectives

---

* The German title has sometimes been translated even more invidiously as *Hucksters and Heroes*.

of Foreign Trade Policy") was used in the writing of *Nation, Staat und Wirtschaft,* which was published in 1919.[1] It was a scientific book with political design. It was an attempt at alienating the affections of the German and Austrian public from National Socialist [Nazi] ideas which then had no special name, and at recommending reconstruction by democratic-liberal policy. My book remained unnoticed and was seldom read. But I know that it will be read in the future. The few friends who are reading it today [1940] do not doubt this.

Toward the end of the war, I published a short essay on the quantity theory in the journal of the Association of Austrian Banks and Bankers, a publication not addressed to the public.[2] My treatment of the inflation problem was not approved by the censor. My tame academic essay was rejected. I had to revise it before it could be published. The next issue immediately carried critical responses, one of which, as far as I can remember, came from bank director Rosenbaum who was financing Federn's *Economist.*

In the summer of 1918 the Army Supreme Command organized a course for officers who were to offer patriotic instructions to the troops. I gave a lecture on "War Costs and War Loans," in which I also tried to oppose the inflationary tendencies.[3] My lecture was published from stenographic notes without giving me the opportunity to read the proofs.

My wartime experiences directed my attention to a problem that appears more important to me every day. Indeed, I should like to call it the primary and fundamental problem of civilization.

Only he who fully understands economic theory can comprehend the great questions of economic and social policy. Only he who masters the most difficult tasks of economics can determine whether capitalism, or socialism, or interventionism constitute suitable systems of social cooperation. However, political decisions are not made by economists, but by public opinion, that is, the people. The majority determines what shall be done. This is true of all systems of government. Even absolute kings and dictators can rule only as public opinion commands.

There are schools of thought that simply do not want to see these problems. Orthodox Marxism believes that the dialectical process of

1. *Nation, State, and Economy,* 1983, 2006.
2. "Zur Währungsfrage," ("On the Question of the Monetary Standard") in *Mitteilungen des Verbandes österreichischer Banken und Bankiers,* 1918. Not available in English.
3. "Über Kriegskostendeckung und Kriegsanleihen" (Vienna: Phoebus, 1918). Not available in English.

historical development guides man unconsciously on his inevitable path, that is, a path toward happiness. Another sort of Marxism believes that the class can never err. Race mysticism maintains the same for the race: the characteristics of the race know how to find the right solution. Religious mysticism, even where it appears in worldly garb, e.g. the Führer principle, depends on God; He will not forsake His children but preserve them through revelation or by sending a blessed Shepherd. But our experience discredits all these escape mechanisms. It reveals that there are different doctrines, different opinions even within the various classes, races, and nations; that different men vie for leadership with different programs; that different churches proclaim their Word of God which disagree among themselves. One would have to be blind to assert that an appeal (1) to the dialectic of history, (2) to an unerring class consciousness, (3) to racial or national characteristics, (4) to God's Word, or (5) a Führer's order, can answer convincingly certain questions, as for example, whether credit expansion really can reduce interest rates permanently.

The liberals of the eighteenth century were filled with a boundless optimism. Mankind is rational, which permits the right opinion to emerge in the end. Light will replace darkness. All the efforts of the advocates of darkness to keep the people in ignorance in order to rule them more easily cannot prevent progress. Thus enlightened by reason, mankind is moving toward ever greater perfection. Democracy with its freedom of thought, speech, and press assures the success of the right doctrine. Let the masses decide; they will choose wisely.

Nobody would now accept this optimism. The conflict of economic doctrines makes far greater demands on our ability to judge than did the problems faced by the Enlightenment: namely (1) the problem of superstition versus natural science, (2) tyranny versus freedom, (3) privilege versus equality before the law.

The people must decide. It is true, economists have the duty to inform their fellowmen. But what happens if these economists do not measure up to the dialectic task and are pushed aside by demagogues? Or if the masses lack the intelligence to understand the teachings of economists? Is not the attempt to guide the people on the right road hopeless, especially when we recognize that men like John Maynard Keynes, Bertrand Russell, Harold Laski and Albert Einstein could not comprehend economic problems?

We fail to understand what is involved, if we expect help from a new election system or an improvement of public education. Technical proposals for changes in the election system would even deny some people the right to participate in the election of a legislature and of an administration. But this would be no solution. If the masses of people oppose an administration that was formed by a minority, it cannot indefinitely survive. If it refuses to yield to public opinion, it will be overthrown by revolution. The preferability of democracy consists in the fact that it facilitates a peaceful adjustment of the system of government and government personnel to the wishes of public opinion, and thus assures peaceful continuation of social cooperation in the state. This is not a problem under democracy only, but much more; it is a problem that exists under all circumstances and every conceivable form of government.

It has been said that the problem lies with public education and information. But we are badly deceived to believe that more schools and lectures, or a popularization of books and journals could promote the right doctrine to victory. In fact, false doctrines can recruit their followers the same way. The evil consists precisely in the people's intellectual disqualifications to choose the means that lead to the desired objectives. The fact that facile decisions can be foisted onto people demonstrates that they are incapable of independent judgment. This is precisely the great danger.

I thus had arrived at this hopeless pessimism that for a long time had burdened the best minds of Europe. We know today from the letters of Jacob Burckhardt that this great historian, too, had no illusions about the future of European civilization. This pessimism had broken the strength of Carl Menger, and it over-shadowed the life of Max Weber. (In the last months of the war Weber lectured for one semester at the University of Vienna, when we became good friends.)

It is a matter of temperament how we shape our lives in the knowledge of an inescapable catastrophe. In high school I had chosen a verse by Virgil as my motto: *Tu ne cede malis sed contra audentior ito* ("Do not yield to the bad, but always oppose it with courage"). In the darkest hours of the war, I recalled this dictum. Again and again I faced situations from which rational deliberations could find no escape. But then something unexpected occurred that brought deliverance. I would not lose courage even now. I would do everything an economist could do. I would not tire in professing what I knew to be right. And so I decided to write a book on socialism which I had contemplated before the war. I now set about executing my old plan.

VIII

With the Chamber of Commerce

Before I proceed with the description of my scientific endeavors, I must return to my practical occupation. From 1909 to 1938 I served the Lower Austrian Chamber of Commerce and Industry. In 1920 the name of this institution was changed to Vienna Chamber of Commerce, Handicrafts and Industry.

In Austria the Chambers were parliamentary bodies that were formed by all businessmen and financed through a surtax on the occupational tax that was collected by the internal revenue service and then transferred to the chambers. They had been created during the year of the 1848 Revolution in order to advise Parliament and government in economic matters, and to assume some administrative functions. They remained rather unimportant until the end of the 1870s. During the 1880s and 1890s they fought in vain against proposed changes that derived from guild ideas, and which were demanded and pushed through by the Christian Social Party. Throughout this time the center of power lay with the General Assembly and the Chamber committees. The office of the Chamber of Commerce merely rendered handy man service.

The breakthrough of the principle of interventionism ushered in a radical change. The secretaries, officials in the departments, and members of Parliament were completely ignorant in economic matters. Most of them had no conception of the consequences of the measures they took, and were even incapable of formulating the laws, decrees, and regulations in such a way that the offices charged with their execution knew what they were expected to do. It was obvious that the Chamber needed pertinent advice and continuous cooperation from men who knew the conditions and were able to do research. The press, Parliament, and the Kaiser blamed the secretaries, who in turn held their departmental officials responsible for daily blunders and their bad consequences. To escape this responsibility the officials were willing to seek the advice of knowledgeable men.

The secretaries of the Vienna Chamber, Rudolf Maresch and Richard Riedl, knew how to use these favorable conditions for an expansion of the influence of the secretary's office. The President of the Chamber at that time was a far-sighted man, Baron Mauthner, who in the House of Deputies played an eminent role as leader of the Mauthner group, named for him. Mauthner agreed to an expansion of the secretary's office, and several young economists were added to the staff. The most eminent among them was my friend, Victor Graetz, a man of unusual gifts and strong character. But just because of his clear perception he suffered from that pessimism from which all knowledgeable men were bound to suffer in these years. The success of this new direction of the Chamber was tremendous; in a short time the secretary's office of the Vienna Chamber became an important factor in economic policy. Its importance grew even further when, under the title *Handelspolitische Zentralstelle* (Center for Trade Policy), it created an organization in which all Austrian Chambers participated. It is true, many Provincial Chambers were rather unimportant as their secretaries were ineffective. But the secretary's offices of Prague, Brno, Reichenberg, Krakow, and Trieste had men whose cooperation was very valuable.

In 1909, continuation of the management of the Vienna Chamber was challenged. Herr Maresch had retired a few years earlier and in 1909 Herr Riedl was appointed head of the trade division of the Department of Commerce. Several young officials had left the Chamber to work in industry, and my friend, Graetz, left in order to assume the management of a large enterprise. He recommended me as his successor.

The Chamber offered me the only field in which I could work in Austria. A university professorship was closed to me inasmuch as the universities were searching for interventionists and socialists. Only those belonging to one of the political parties—the Christian Social Party, German National Party, or the Social Democratic Party—could hope for an appointment. Nor did I aspire to a position in government service. After the war my reputation as an expert in both money and banking was so extensively recognized that several big banks offered me a position on their boards. But until 1921 I always declined for the reason that they refused to give assurance that my advice would be followed; after 1921 I declined because I considered all banks insolvent and irretrievably lost. Events bore me out.

In the Chamber I created a position for myself. Officially I was never more than an employee in the secretary's office; I always had a nominal superior under whom I worked, together with a few colleagues. I never had the desire to assume the management and use some of my productive strength for administrative routine. My position was incomparably greater than that of any other Chamber official or any Austrian who did not preside over one of the big political parties. I was the economist of the country.

This does not mean that my recommendations were followed or that my warnings were heeded. Supported only by a few friends I waged a hopeless fight. All I achieved was to delay the catastrophe. The fact that in the winter of 1918–1919 Bolshevism did not take over and that the collapse of industry and banks did not occur in 1921, but in 1931, was in large part the result of my efforts. More could not be attained, or at least not by me.

Not all of the Chamber's operations had my approval. I did not participate in the purely administrative work. All my strength was concentrated on the crucial economic political questions.

Occasionally I was reproached because I made my point too bluntly and intransigently, and I was told that I could have achieved more if I had shown more willingness to compromise. The Secretary General of the Central Association of Austrian Industry, Gustav Weiss von Wellenstein, an old friend, often reproached me. I felt the criticism was unjustified; I could be effective only if I presented the situation truthfully as I saw it. As I look back today at my activity with the Chamber I regret only my willingness to compromise, not my intransigence. I was always ready to yield in unimportant matters if I could save other more important issues. Occasionally I even made intellectual compromises by signing reports which included statements that did not represent my position. This was the only possible way to gain acceptance by the General Assembly of the Chamber or approval by the public of matters I considered very important. If anyone should ever study the published progress and business reports of archives of the Chamber, he would find confirmation of my statement. The reports, opinions, and petitions which carry my name as reporting officer I did not look upon as *my* work, but expressions of opinion of the institution for which

I worked. I always drew a sharp distinction between my scientific and my political activity. In science, compromises are treason to truth. In politics, compromises are unavoidable because results can be achieved only through compromise of conflicting opinion. Science is the creation of individuals; it is never the achievement of the cooperation of a number of people. The essence of politics, though, is cooperation and thus often requires compromises.

In the Austria of the postwar period I was the economic conscience. Only a few helped me and all political parties distrusted me. And yet, all secretaries and party leaders sought my advice and opinion. I never tried to press my opinion on them. I never sought out a statesman or politician. Unless I was formally invited I never appeared in the lobbies of Parliament and government departments. Secretaries and party leaders visited my Chamber office more often than I visited theirs.

I enjoyed the cooperation of my colleagues in the Chamber. Some of them were men of great intelligence and knowledge who strongly promoted my endeavors.

My activity with the Chamber greatly enlarged my horizon. I saw a great deal. That I today [1940] have the material for a social and economic history of the decline of Austrian culture is largely the result of the studies I pursued working for the Chamber. I gathered a great deal of knowledge from my journeys that took me to all parts of old Austria-Hungary. From 1912 to 1914 I investigated the industrial situation with regard to the renewal of the customs union and trade relations with Hungary, and to the adoption of new autonomous tariffs and trade treaties.

But my efforts in the Chamber were not mainly directed at commercial problems, but rather at finance, currency, credit, and tax policy. Again and again I was assigned special tasks. Between the Armistice [in 1918] and the signing of the peace agreement at Saint Germain I was the authority on financial matters pertaining to foreign affairs. Later, when the terms of the peace treaty were put into effect I was in charge of the office that dealt with prewar debt. In this position I had to negotiate frequently with the representatives of our former enemies. I was Austrian delegate to the International Chamber of Commerce and member of many international commissions and committees, whose insoluble task it was to facilitate peaceful exchange of goods and services in a world that was animated by national hatred and preparing for genocide.

In 1926, I founded the Austrian Institute for Business Cycle Research. Together with Dollfuss[1] and Palla, the Secretary of the Chamber of Labor, I belonged to the publication committee of the Economic Commission which in 1931, with the cooperation of Professor Richard Schüller, published *"Bericht über die wirtschaftlichen Schwierigkeiten Österreichs"* ("Report on the Economic Difficulties of Austria").

I need not say more about the various activities that consumed my time with the Chamber. It was hard work, often consisting of many useless trifles. But this is uninteresting. Let me talk about my political objectives that gave direction to my work.

My political activity from 1918 to 1934 can be divided into four parts:

Prevention of Bolshevist Takeover
Halting the Inflation
Avoidance of Banking Crisis
Struggle Against Takeover by Germany

Prevention of Bolshevist Takeover

During the first period, from the collapse of the Monarchy in the fall of 1918 to the fall of 1919, the most important task I had set for myself was the prevention of a Bolshevist takeover. I have already mentioned that I succeeded in that through my influence with Otto Bauer. It was solely due to my efforts that Bolshevism did not then prevail in Vienna. Only a few people had supported me in my efforts and their help was rather ineffective. I, alone, managed to turn Bauer away from seeking union with Moscow. The radical young men who rejected Bauer's authority and were eager to proceed alone and against the will of the Party leadership were so inexperienced, incapable, and torn by mutual rivalry that they could not even form a half-way viable communist party organization. The events lay in the hands of the leaders of the old Social Democratic Party, where Bauer had the final word.

Halting the Inflation

When this danger had passed, I directed all my efforts toward halting the inflation. In this fight I had found an excellent comrade. Wilhelm

---

1. Englebert Dollfuss, Chancellor of Austria, 1932–34, assassinated by the Austrian Nazis in 1934.

Rosenberg had been one of Carl Menger's students and in true friendship had remained faithful to his old teacher. He was a sharp thinker, excellent economist, and brilliant jurist. As an attorney he had excelled in such a way that his advice was sought in all difficult questions of business and finance. He enjoyed the highest prestige as "expert" in financial questions, and was willing to use this prestige in the fight against inflation.

We fought three years before we achieved our goal—restoration of a balanced budget and cessation of any further increase of bank notes. It was to our merit alone that the Austrian crown was finally stabilized at a ratio of 14,400 paper crowns to one gold crown, and not at higher rates. But this was not the result we actually sought.

If it had not been for our passionate agitation against the continuation of the deficit and inflation policy, the crown in early 1922 would have fallen to one-millionth or one-billionth of its gold parity of 1892. It probably would have been impossible for any administration to maintain public order. Foreign troops would have had to occupy the country and foreign powers would have built a new state. This catastrophe was avoided. It was an Austrian administration that eliminated the deficit and stabilized the crown. The Austrian currency did not collapse like the German currency in 1923. The crackup boom did not occur. Nevertheless, the country for many years had to suffer from the destructive consequences of continuous inflation. Its banking, credit and insurance systems had suffered wounds that could no longer heal. The consumption of capital could not be halted. We met too much resistance; our victory came too late. It delayed the ultimate collapse by several years, but could no longer save Austria.

Rosenberg and I suffered no illusions about that. We knew what the stabilization actually meant. My friend succumbed to the pessimism of hopelessness, the fate of all enlightened Austrians. It was not only the grief of having lost his only son, but also the knowledge that all his work and effort were without hope of success that drove him to his death.

Avoidance of Banking Crisis

Our success in the struggle for a balanced budget was delayed because we met so much opposition in convincing the Christian Social Party of the necessity to eliminate subsidies which the state was paying toward a reduction in the price of foodstuffs. Such a reduction played a minor role in the budget of consumers, but it prevented the restoration of balance in the government budget. With the help of Weiss-Wellenstein we succeeded in persuading big industry to grant concessions to the labor unions in case the food subsidies ceased. The fact that the labor unions agreed to our plan behind the back of the Social Democratic Party leadership was a serious blow to the leaders of the Party. To disrupt the negotiations, Otto Bauer took desperate measures; on December 1, 1921, the "organizers," that is, the Social Democratic Party troops, invaded the inner city and plundered and demolished all retail stores. Determined to stay "neutral" politically, the police did not interfere. But in the coming days public opinion was aroused against such tactics. The Social Democrats had to retreat, and the negotiations with the labor unions could continue.

We must not underestimate the merit which the leader of the Christian Social Party, Professor Seipel, manifested in those days.[2] Seipel's ignorance in economic affairs was that which only a cleric could have. He saw inflation as an evil, but otherwise was rather unacquainted with financial policy. Rosenberg and I felt obligated to inform him that a currency stabilization would soon reveal the consequences of inflation, in the form of a "stabilization crisis." And we explained to him that public opinion would blame the stabilizer for the depression that would follow the inflation boom. The Christian Social Party could expect no gratitude, only complaints!

Professor Seipel greatly appreciated our sincerity. A useful and necessary measure must be undertaken, he believed, even if it would harm the Party. The statesman differs from the demagogue in that he prefers right over that which brings applause. There were not many politicians in Austria who thought that way. I have felt the highest respect for the high and honest character of this noble priest whose world view and conception of life remained alien to me. He was a great personality.

Unfortunately Seipel's ignorance in the ways of the world inflicted great harm on his Party. He just did not see the corruption of the Christian Social and German National Party members who were his colleagues. He did not notice that his Party friends were striving for personal enrichment only.

2. Monsignor Ignaz Seipel, Roman Catholic prelate and statesman, Chancellor of Austria, 1922–1924, 1926–1929, and Minister of Foreign Affairs, 1930.

These Party friends, especially Deputy Victor Kienböck the attorney, who later became Minister of Finance and then President of the National Bank, had introduced Seipel to Gottfried Kunwald. Herr Kunwald, who was the son of an eminent Viennese attorney, was a cripple from birth. With the greatest effort only he could walk a few steps; he had to hobble from room to room, which meant he was in need of constant care and attention. Two strong men always accompanied him, lifting him in and out of the car, carrying him up or down the steps. But in spite of these handicaps Kunwald had bravely completed his education and earned a Doctor of Law degree. Admission to the bar was denied him since his physical condition did not permit him to complete the required one-year practice at court. But he was working in the attorney's office founded by his father and continued by his brother-in-law. As an excellent and knowledgeable jurist he had a wide clientele.

Herr Kunwald had read a great deal, but he could not think in economic terms. He saw economic problems with the eyes of a jurist only, who must prepare contracts. He was a foe of inflation because as a jurist he saw the harm it did to the economy. When Rosenberg and I launched our fight against inflation, he was willing to support us, in his way.

He enjoyed the boundless confidence of several Christian Social politicians and bankers whom he had advised in difficult legal matters. The transactions of these friends of Kunwald were not always beyond reproach. Ruthlessly using their positions in public life, these Christian Social politicians secured all kinds of orders, assisted procurement of government contracts, exerted influence in all government agencies, for a commission. During the inflation they had thus profited greatly and now were afraid that a stabilization would jeopardize their interests. But Kunwald informed them that in any case the inflation boom would soon come to an end, and he intimated that he would find new opportunities for profit for them after the stabilization.

When Rosenberg and I succeeded in winning Professor Seipel and his Party over to monetary stabilization, they elected Kunwald as their confidant for taking the necessary measures. He proved himself to be most capable and was completely equal to the task. In general, we could work with him rather well. During our fight for stabilization he had gathered around him a circle of bankers, government officials, and Christian Social politicians with whom he conducted a kind of financial political seminar. But several years later, as he continued this activity, his influence became damaging. He spent much time trying to refute or weaken my critique of the prevailing interventionist policy. According to him, interventionism was not so bad as I presented it; Austria was making economic progress, and it would be absurd to believe that interventionist policies achieve nothing but capital consumption.

I know, without doubt, that Kunwald lacked good faith when he presented his optimism. He saw the true situation of the banks and big enterprises and occasionally made remarks that were no less pessimistic than mine. But he was convinced that to present the plain truth about the state of affairs would diminish his influence with the secretaries, through whom he secured licenses and other favors for his clients, and thus jeopardize his income as an attorney and financial agent.

It was extraordinarily difficult to counteract Kunwald's unfavorable influence. In public these things could not be freely discussed, as the credit reputation of the Austrian economy had to be protected with care. It would have been very easy, indeed, to present the facts in such a way that everyone would have seen the necessity for halting the policy of capital consumption, but such action would have undermined the banks' foreign credit thereby making instant bankruptcy unavoidable. Therefore, I was forced to use extraordinary restraint in my efforts to change economic policies lest I frighten the public and jeopardize the credit of banks and industry. This restraint guided my conduct during the third period from the crown stabilization in 1922 to the collapse of the *Kreditanstalt* in the spring of 1931. The worse the situation grew through the continuation of the disastrous policy, the greater became the danger of a credit crisis and the more important it became not to disquiet the foreign markets. After the collapse of the *Bodenkreditanstalt* in 1929, I, myself, insisted that graphic presentations of the progress that was made by industry in Austria after 1922 be shown at a London exhibit. It was clear to me and to Friedrich von Hayek, who as head of the Institute for Trade Cycle Research had prepared the tables, that this progress was rather questionable. However, using only data that were unobjectionable statistically, the tables showed progress within the prevailing mercantilistic view. Therefore, I could see no harm in showing them abroad.

With all due consideration for the precarious credit situation, I never embellished the description of conditions, nor tolerated a suppression or even falsification of statistical data. For the economic commission mentioned in the foregoing I had the Institute prepare an investigation into capital consumption. When the publication committee planned to publish the results of this investigation in its report, the banks raised objections. I knew then already that the great banking crisis was close at hand, and therefore endeavored to avoid everything that could hasten its coming. The objections of the banks were unfounded, but I agreed to publication under the condition that neither the economic commission nor the Institute should publish the results; it was therefore published by the head of the Institute, Oskar Morgenstern, under his own name.

My labor, during this third period of my political activity in postwar Austria, was even more routine than during the earlier periods. It was petty, detailed labor in a daily fight against ignorance, inability, indolence, malice, and corruption. I was not alone in this fight. Dear good friends assisted me, especially Siegfried Strakosch von Feldringen, Gustav Weiss von Wellenstein and Victor Graetz. The help I received from my assistant, Therese Wolf-Thieberger, was especially valuable for my work in the Chamber. Her extraordinary intelligence, her cheerfulness in work, and her personal courage supported me in many dark hours.

Struggle Against Takeover by Germany

In all these years the slogan of the "incapability" of Austria exerted its pernicious influence. In Austria and abroad everyone was convinced that Austria was not "fit to survive." It was believed that a "small" country could not stay independent, especially if it must import important raw materials. Therefore, Austria should seek merger with a larger economic unit, such as the German Reich.

Outside Austria even those circles that had added the annexation prohibition to the peace treaty of Saint Germain held to this belief. To facilitate political independence for Austria they recommended special economic privileges. The international loan in connection with Seipel's crown stabilization in 1922 was granted for this reason. Austria did not then need a foreign loan; it needed a finance commissioner who was a foreigner. The government needed the opportunity to shift to a foreigner the responsibility, and thereby the odium, of vetoing an increase in outlays. The League of Nations appointed as finance commissioner an ignorant, tactless and arrogant Dutchman by the name of Zimmermann. In his name an official of the Ministry of Finance,

Hans Patzauer, conducted the business. Herr Patzauer, highly gifted, firm in character, and very knowledgeable, discharged his obligations very well. At the age of less than fifty he died a short time before the expiration of the Zimmermann mission. How essential this financial supervision of the Austrian state really was became evident a few hours after its termination, when the government guaranteed the obligations of the *Zentralbank Deutscher Sparkassen,* an insolvent bank.

Besides the granting of this League of Nations loan and of another one in 1932, the Western powers did nothing to assist Austria. When the Nazis made it difficult to export Austrian lumber to Germany, the French government was petitioned in vain to grant tariff reductions on lumber exports to France.

In the eyes of the German Nationalists, who since the collapse of the monarchy called themselves the party for a "Greater Germany," the fiction of the incapability of Austria to survive was a cogent argument for the annexation. For the Christian Social Party, who pretended to favor the annexation but actually did everything to prevent it, the legend was a convenient excuse for sabotaging all attempts at a reasonable economic policy. We are incapable of surviving anyway, they would say. Therefore, it is useless to search for an economic policy that could give vitality to our country. In fact, they considered it almost unpatriotic to propose reforms that would improve the economic situation. The theory of the incapability of Austria to survive was seen as the most important asset of foreign policy. With this theory, they thought they could obtain many kinds of favors from the Western powers. Anyone who criticized the idea of incapability to survive publicly, as for instance Friedrich Otto Hertz did, thereby was viewed as a traitor.

It is not necessary to demonstrate how unsustainable this doctrine of the incapability of small countries to survive actually is. But I would like to point out how contradictory the appeal to this doctrine was by the protectionists who came into power. Industry in postwar Austria [after large territorial losses] suffered less from the dissolution of the tariff union of the old monarchy, than did industry in the Sudetenland [Czechoslovakia]. After 1918 several Austrian industries, freed from the pressures of Sudetenland competition, were able to expand their production. Other industries, as for instance many branches of the textile industry, came into existence only then in Austria. In the old tariff union, Austrian agriculture had a difficult position in relation to Hungarian agriculture. Now, thanks to a prohibitive trade policy, Austria could greatly expand its production. The fact that Austria had to import coal was no disadvantage due to the depressed prices in the coal market. Above all, it should be borne in mind that during the Great Depression that began in 1929 the prices of raw materials fell faster and farther than those of industrial products. The depression hit the agricultural and raw material countries harder than the industrial countries. It was therefore unjustified for Austria to join in the complaints about the fall of raw material prices.

Also financially, the new Austria suffered less from the dissolution of the old [Austro-Hungarian] empire than did its other parts. In the old empire the government had used some of the Austrian tax revenues to cover the administrative costs of its other divisions. Formerly the old Austria in the empire had not lived on revenues from other divisions, e.g. on those from Galicia or Dalmatia, but had on the contrary subsidized the latter.

It has been said that Austria had to assume a disproportionate share of the inherited administration cost of the old empire. That, too, is incorrect. The new Austria inherited a small number of civil servants, mostly employees of the state-owned railroad, who had been working in other parts of the monarchy. Their precise number could never be ascertained as the officials would foil any attempt at finding out. But there cannot be any doubt that far fewer than one thousand civil servants were involved. At the same time, many thousands—even tens of thousands—of new people were engaged in the new Austria, especially by the railroad. The surplus of government officials in the new Austria had nothing to do with the legacy of the old empire.

The paralyzing effect of the catchword, "incapability of survival," cannot be overstated. Wherever a reform proposal emerged, it was rejected immediately on grounds of this catchword. The notorious inefficiency, the calamitous "nothing can be done" (*da lasst sich nix machen*), all found their common justification in that catchword.

This situation sometimes made me vacillate in my position on the annexation program. I was not blind regarding the danger to Austrian culture in a union with the German Reich. But there were moments in which I asked myself whether the annexation was not a lesser evil than the continuation of a policy that inescapably had to lead to catastrophe.

Since the currency reform in 1922, Austria was formally ruled by a coalition of the Christian Social Party and the Party for a Greater Germany. The Social Democrats were the opposition party blaming the "bourgeois" parties for all defects of the existing system. In reality the situation was quite different. The center of executive power rested in the hands of individual state governments, which were elected by the state legislatures. The power of the new central state, namely, the new federal parliament and government, was rather limited. In the most important, most populous and richest state, the city of Vienna, the Social Democratic Party ruled autocratically. It used this power to wage a ruthless war of destruction against the capitalist order. The next important state, Lower Austria, was ruled by a coalition of Social Democrats and the Christian Social Party, where the Greater Germans formed the opposition. In the third-most important state, Styria, the Social Democrats again participated in the government. Only in the smaller, financially poorer and less populous states did the Social Democrats stand in opposition.

But the real power of the Social Democratic Party did not rest in its parliamentary representation and its participation in government, but rather in its terror apparatus. The Party ruled all labor unions, especially the unions of railroad, postal service, telegraph, and telephone employees. At any time the Party could paralyze, through strike, all economic life. As soon as the Party disapproved of a position of the federal government, it threatened a strike in production requisite for survival, which caused the government to yield.

It was even more significant that the Social Democratic Party had at its disposal a Party army that was equipped with rifles and machine guns—even with light artillery and ample ammunition—an army with manpower at least three times greater than the government troops, such as the federal forces, state, and local police. The federal forces possessed neither tanks, nor heavy artillery, nor airplanes, all of which were prohibited by the peace treaty, the disarmament provisions of which were strictly supervised by the military attachés of the Western powers. Toward the Social Democrats they were more lenient. During the months that followed the Armistice and the ratification of the peace treaty, they permitted Social Democrats to remove from the supplies of the old army as much war material and ammunition as they could and cared to take. Later the Social Democrats were permitted to acquire supplies of weapons and ammunition from Czechoslovakia. The Social Democratic Army, officially called the "Organizers," conducted open marches and field exercises which the government was unable to oppose. Unchallenged, the Party claimed the "right to the street."

Earlier the Social Democrats had extorted this right by force in the old empire. During the commotion that in 1907 led to the adoption of universal, equal, and direct suffrage for the Austrian Parliament, the Social Democratic Party attempted to intimidate and bring government and Parliament to heel through terror. The Austrian constitution had expressly prohibited public outdoor meetings during the sessions and in the vicinity of Parliament, which was to assure that decisions could be made without consideration of the public temper in the capital. Anyway, before 1907 the city of Vienna had more delegates in Parliament than corresponded to the size of its population. Nevertheless, the Social Democrats did not heed the prohibition against intimidation, and the Imperial Government tolerated it. On November 28, 1905, Vienna was completely paralyzed and 250,000 workers marched on Ringstrasse past Parliament in military fashion in rows of eight, under the leadership of Party officials. That evening I happened to meet Otto Bauer in a coffeehouse. He was quite inebriated by the success of this demonstration and proclaimed with great satisfaction that the Social Democratic Party had achieved "street autonomy," which it would know how to defend forever. Being of different opinion I asked him: "What will happen if some day another party attains street autonomy with organized force? Would this not lead to civil war?" Bauer's answer was quite characteristic:

> Only a bourgeois could raise this question, a bourgeois who does not realize that the future belongs to us [the Socialists] alone. Where is such a party to come from which could dare to confront the organized proletariat? Once we have come to power, there will be no more resistance.

Marxism made the Social Democrats blind and stupid. During the early years of the Austrian Republic I once heard the Social Democratic Mayor Seitz remark:

> The rule of the Social Democratic Party in Vienna is now assured forever. Already in kindergarten the child acquires proletarian consciousness. The school teaches Social Democracy and labor unions complete this education. The Viennese is born into the Social Democracy, he lives in it and dies as he has lived.

I incurred the displeasure of all those present when I limited my reply to a Viennese idiom: "*Es sollen auch schon vierstöckige Hausherren gestorben sein*" ("Even some high and mighty [should] have died").

The terror caused by the Social Democrats forced other Austrians to build their defenses. Attempts were made as early as winter 1918–1919. After various failures, the "Home Guard" had some organizational success. But until 1934 its financial support and the number of its members remained rather modest, and rivalries between its leaders blunted its strength.

I watched with horror this development that indeed was unavoidable. It was obvious that Austria was moving toward civil war. I could not prevent it. Even my best friends held to the opinion that the force [actual and threatened] of the Social Democratic Party could be opposed only by violence.

The formation of the Home Guard introduced a new type of individual into politics. Adventurers without education and desperados with narrow horizons became the leaders, because they were good at drill and had a loud voice to give commands. Their bible was the manual of arms; their slogan, "authority." These adventurers—petty *Il Duces* and *Führers*—identified democracy with Social Democracy and therefore looked upon democracy "as the worst of all evils." Later they clung to the catch-word, "corporate state" ("*Ständestaat*"). Their social ideal was a military state in which they alone would command [be the man on horseback].

With the collapse of the *Kreditanstalt** in May 1931, the third phase of my activity with the Chamber came to a close. Now only a narrow scope for action remained. With all the strength at my disposal I opposed the inflationary policy upon which the government had again embarked. That the inflation went no further than to 175 Austrian shillings (from 139) for 100 Swiss francs and that very soon new stabilization was achieved at this rate of exchange was my achievement alone.

But the fight for Austria remained lost. Even if I had been completely successful, Austria could not have been saved. The enemy who was about to destroy it came from abroad [Hitler's Nazi Germany]. Austria could not for long withstand the onslaught of the National Socialists who soon were to overrun all of Europe.

The problems for Austria were no longer primarily domestic. Her fate lay in the hands of Western Europe. Whoever wanted to work for Austria had to do so abroad. When in the spring of 1934 I was offered

---

* Major banking institution in Austria, the collapse of which sharply worsened the whole world's already bad financial and monetary structure.

the chair for International Relations with the Institut Universitaire des Hautes Etudes Internationales (Graduate Institute of International Studies), I accepted with delight. I retained my position with the Chamber of Commerce and occasionally returned to Vienna in order to continue my old activity. But I was determined not to move back to Vienna until after the destruction of the Nazi Reich. I shall discuss my political activity between 1934 and 1938 in the following chapters.

For sixteen years I fought a battle in the Chamber in which I won nothing more than a mere delay of the catastrophe. I made heavy personal sacrifices although I always foresaw that success would be denied me. But I do not regret that I attempted the impossible. I could not act otherwise. I fought because I could do no other.

My Teaching Activities in Vienna

To me no other vocation seemed more attractive than that of a university teacher. I recognized rather early that as a classical liberal a full professorship at a university in German-speaking countries would always be denied me. I regretted this only because it forced me to earn my living through nonacademic work. A position as an unsalaried lecturer (*Privatdozent*) appeared to me to be an effective opportunity for salutary teaching.

In 1913 I had been admitted to the faculty of law at the University of Vienna as an unsalaried lecturer, and in the spring of 1918 I received the title of Associate Professor. I did not go any further in my academic career in Austria. I am sure that in 1938 the Nazis dropped me from the list of lecturers, although they did not trouble themselves to inform me about it.

During the early years of my academic activity I did some lecturing. Later I limited myself to conducting a two-hour seminar on problems of economic theory. The success of this teaching burgeoned from year to year. Nearly all students who took seriously the study of economics attended my seminar. It is true, this was merely a small percentage of the many hundreds of students who every year obtained their doctor's degrees in either law or in the social sciences. But my seminars were overcrowded. Customarily a seminar does not have more than twenty to twenty-five members; I regularly had forty to fifty.

After Wieser's retirement and Grünberg's move to Frankfurt, the three professorships of economics were held by Othmar Spann, Hans Mayer and Count Ferdinand Degenfeld-Schonburg. Spann barely knew modern economics; he did not teach economics, he preached a "universalism," i.e., national socialism. Degenfeld did not have the slightest notion of the problems of economics; the level of his instruction would have been scarcely satisfactory for a low-ranking commercial college. Mayer was the favorite pupil of Wieser. He knew the works of Wieser and also those of Böhm-Bawerk and Menger. He, himself, was totally without critical faculty, never manifested independent thought, and basically never comprehended what it was all about in economics. The awareness of his sterility and incapability depressed him badly, and made him unstable and malicious. He occupied his time with an open fight against Professor Spann and with mischievous intrigues against me. His lectures were miserable, his seminar not much better. I need not be proud of the fact that the students, young doctors and the numerous foreigners who studied in Vienna for one or two semesters, preferred my instruction.

Professors Spann and Mayer were jealous of my success and sought to alienate my students from me. In major examinations, my students reported that there was discrimination against them, something which I could not prove (investigate). But I always told the members of my seminar that I attached no great importance to their official registration. They frequently made use of this permission. Of the forty to fifty who attended, only eight to ten usually had registered. The professors also made it very difficult for those doctoral candidates in the social sciences who wanted to write their theses with me; and those who sought to qualify for a university lectureship had to be careful not to be known as my students.

Students who registered for my seminar were denied access to the library of the economics department if they did not also register for a seminar of one of the three professors. Such measures completely missed their mark; I had collected an excellent library in the Chamber of Commerce which, especially in modern Anglo-Saxon literature, was incomparably better than that of the University economics department.

All such matters did not disturb me. It was much more serious that the general level of instruction at the University of Vienna was so low. The brilliance that had marked the University during my student years had long been lost. Many professors could not even be called educated men. The School of Law and the School of Fine Arts were permeated by a spirit that was alien to culture and science. During the first half of the 1920s I was invited occasionally to the discussions of prominent professors, the topic of which was increasing the budget appropriations by the state. I was invited because they counted on my support with Financial Counsellor Herr Patzauer, and the associate of Commissioner Zimmermann. In one of the discussions a letter by a foreign friend of Viennese culture was read, in which appeared the terms, "pragmatism," "behaviorism," and "revival." It then became apparent that no one present had ever heard those terms. On another occasion it became clear that the name "Benedetto Croce" was unknown to all and that the name of "Henri Bergson" was unknown to most. Among the participants in these discussions were the President of the Academy of Sciences, Oswald Redlich, who was the Professor of Medieval History, and Count Wenzel Gleisbach, Professor of Criminal Law.

One can thus imagine the average educational level of students. In the master's examinations in the social sciences I was the examiner on economics and finance. The ignorance which the candidates revealed was crushing. But it was even worse that the members of the examination committee were not distressed by this failure. I remember that I had a hard time persuading the committee to flunk a candidate who believed (1) that Marx had lived during the eighteenth century, (2) that the tax on beer was a direct tax and who, in his examination on public law, revealed (3) that he had no idea of the concept of "Ministerial accountability of members of the Cabinet." It is true, I learned later that such ignorance was to be found also in the very highest places. The President of Austria, Miklas, who had been teacher of history in a secondary school, once had a discussion with me and the President of the Central Bank, Professor Richard Reisch, on the most-favored-nation clause. During the conversation I mentioned the Peace of Frankfurt. President Miklas then inquired when and between what countries that peace treaty had been concluded [between France and Germany in 1871].

There was an unbridgeable gap in Austria between an infinitesimally small number of Viennese intellectuals, on the one hand, and the masses of so-called educated people, on the other. The educational system was so inadequate that an education could really not be imparted to young people. The majority of doctors of law, of the social sciences, and of philosophy were trained inadequately for their profession, were unable to think, and avoided reading serious books. Of one hundred Viennese attorneys at law no more than ten could read a journal in English or French. Outside Vienna and with jurists in public service the situation was even worse.

As an official of the Chamber of Commerce I had to cope with these conditions. As a teacher I met with only a select few of the most gifted. Even in 1906 to 1912, when I taught economics to the senior class of the Vienna Commercial Academy for girls, and during the academic year 1918–1919 at the Vienna Export Academy (later, Institute for World Trade) when I offered a course for officers who sought to enter civilian life, I mostly dealt with students who were better than average.

My main teaching effort was focused on my *Privatseminar*. Beginning in 1920, during the months of October to June, a number of young people gathered around me once every two weeks. My office in the Chamber of Commerce was spacious enough to accommodate twenty to twenty-five persons. We usually met at seven in the evening and adjourned at ten-thirty. In these meetings we informally discussed all important problems of economics, social philosophy, sociology, logic, and the epistemology of the sciences of human action. In this circle the younger* Austrian School of Economics lived on; in this circle the Viennese culture produced one of its last blossoms. Here I was neither teacher nor director of seminar. I was merely *primus inter pares* (first among peers) who himself benefited more than he gave.

All who belonged to this circle came voluntarily, guided only by their thirst for knowledge. They came as pupils, but over the years became my friends. Several of my contemporaries later joined the circle. Foreign scholars visiting Vienna were welcome guests and actively participated in the discussions.

My *Privatseminar* had no official meaning or function. It was connected neither with the University nor with the Chamber. It was and always remained the circle of my much younger friends. Outsiders knew nothing of our meetings; they merely saw the works that were published by the participants.

We formed neither school, congregation, nor sect. We helped each other more through contradiction than agreement. But we agreed and were united on one endeavor: to further the sciences of human action. Each one went his own way, guided by his own law. We never organized or undertook anything that resembled the nauseous "carrying on" of the German Imperial and postwar "scientists." We never gave thought to publishing a journal or a collection of essays. Each one worked by himself, as it befits a thinker. And yet, each one of us labored

---

* The Austrian School of Economics *after* Menger and Böhm-Bawerk.

for the circle, seeking no compensation other than simple recognition, not the applause of his friends. There was greatness in this unpretentious exchange of ideas; in it we all found happiness and satisfaction.

Besides this *Privatseminar* there was yet another association of the friends of economic inquiry. Since March 12, 1908, Karl Pribram, Emil Perels, Else Cronbach, and I had arranged regular meetings for the discussion of economic problems and basic questions in related sciences. The circle soon grew; the beautiful conference room of the Central Association for Housing Reform provided a dignified setting. During the war, when I was absent from Vienna, the admission of new members was handled rather carelessly, which impaired the appropriate character of the discussions. When I returned to Vienna, the meetings had been discontinued. Immediately after the war I sought to revive the group. But in order to avoid any conflict with the authorities we had to draw up a formal association, which we called the "Economic Society." We soon ran into difficulties once more when we discovered that cooperation with Professor Spann was impossible. After a while we succeeded in relieving ourselves of Professor Spann, and the Society resumed its activity.

Anyone demonstrating genuine interest in economic problems could be elected to be a member of the Society. At irregular intervals we conducted evening meetings in the Conference Room of the Banking Association. Society members or out-of-town guests gave lectures that were always followed by lively discussion. The participants of my *Privatseminar* formed the nucleus of membership; but there were also several other excellent economists, such as Richard Schüller, Siegfried Strakosch von Feldringen, Victor Graetz, and many others.

As the Economic Society did not want to irritate the University professors, it felt obliged to make Hans Mayer [the Wieser favorite] its President. I served as Vice President. In 1934, when I left for Geneva and returned for short visits only, the Society slowly began to die.

On March 19, 1938, Hans Mayer wrote to all its members as follows:

> In consideration of the changed situation in German Austria I am informing you that under the respective laws now applicable also to this state, all non-Aryan members are leaving the Economic Society.

[The underlying reason for this was the anti-Semitic policy of the Nazis.]

This was the last that was heard of the Economic Society.

Regular participants in the *Privatseminar** were:
Ludwig Bettelheim-Gabillon
Victor Bloch
Stephanie Braun-Browne
Friedrich Engel von Janosi
Walter Froehlich
Gottfried von Haberler
Friedrich A. von Hayek
Marianne von Herzfeld
Felix Kaufmann
Rudolf Klein
Helene Lieser-Berger
Rudolf Loebl
Gertrud Lovasy
Fritz Machlup
Ilse Mintz-Schüller
Oskar Morgenstern
Elly Offenheimer-Spiro
Adolf G. Redlich-Redley
Paul N. Rosenstein-Rodan
Karol Schlesinger
Fritz Schreier
Alfred Schütz
Richard von Strigl
Erich Voegelin
Robert Wälder
Emanuel Winternitz

---

* About the Mises *Privatseminar*, see also Gottfried von Haberler's delightful description in the appendixes of Mises's *Planning for Freedom,* Memorial Edition, 1974, Libertarian Press, South Holland, Illinois, pages 190 to 192.

X

Scientific Work in Germany

The *Verein für Socialpolitik* (Association for Social Policy) held its 1909 meetings in Vienna and its 1911 meetings in Nuremberg. I participated in both as a silent observer. At the 1919 convention in Regensburg I was elected a member of the Committee, something which did not mean much as it was a customary honor bestowed on all contributors to Association publications. But over the years my position in the Association grew in importance. In contrast to its policy before World War I, the Association sought representatives of all schools of thought. And as I was recognized as a representative of the Austrian School, activity in the Association engaged me more and more. Finally, I was elected to the Board of Directors of the Association. I participated in the preparation of the publications on the cartel problem. The preparation and conduct of the debates on the problem of economic value, held in 1932 in Dresden, were mainly my work.

I was elected a member of the German Association for Sociology in (I think) 1924 or 1925. In 1933 I withdrew from both organizations.

The impression I gained of the German university professors of the "economic state sciences" and sociology was not favorable. True, there were a number of sincere, educated men who were genuinely desirous of scientific inquiry. But most of them were not.

That these men were no economists we must not hold against them. After all, they were the pupils of Schmoller, Wagner, Bücher and Brentano. They did not know the economic literature, had no conception of economic problems, and suspected every economist as an enemy of the State, as non-German, and as protagonists of business interests and of free trade. Whenever they examined an economic essay, they were determined to find deficiencies and errors. They were dilettantes in everything they undertook. They pretended to be historians, but they scarcely looked at the collaborative sciences, which are the most important tools of the historian. The spirit of historical research was alien to them. They were unaware of the basic mathematical problems in the use of statistics. They were laymen in jurisprudence, technology, banking, and trade techniques. With amazing unconcern they published books and essays on things of which they understood nothing.

It was much more serious that they were always ready to turn with the wind. In 1918 most of them sympathized with the Social Democrats; in 1933 they joined the Nazis. If Bolshevism had come to power, they would have become communists.

Werner Sombart was the great master of this set. He was known as a pioneer in economic history, economic theory, and sociology. And he enjoyed a reputation as an independent man, because he had once aroused Kaiser Wilhelm's anger. Professor Sombart really deserved the recognition of his colleagues because to the greatest degree he combined in his person all their shortcomings. He never knew any ambition other than to draw attention to himself and to make money. His imposing work on modern capitalism is a historical monstrosity. He was always seeking public applause. He wrote paradoxes because he could then count on success. He was highly gifted, but at no time did he endeavor to think and work seriously. Of the occupational disease of German professors—delusions of grandeur—he had acquired an elephantine share. When it was fashionable to be a Marxian, he professed Marxism; when Hitler came to power, he wrote that the Führer receives his orders from God!

Concerning economics, Professor Sombart manifested no interest whatsoever. In about 1922 when Weiss-Wellenstein asked him in my presence to give a lecture on inflation, he declined with the words: "That is a problem of bank technique which does not interest me, because it has nothing to do with economics." He had planned to give his book, *Die drei Nationalökonomien* (*The Three Systems of Economics**), another title: *Das Ende der Nationalökonomie* (*The Death of Economics*). He told me that it was only out of consideration for his colleagues, who were earning a livelihood from teaching economics, that he refrained from doing so.

And yet, it was more stimulating to talk to Sombart than to most other professors. At least he was not stupid and obtuse.

* Availability in English unknown.

Several professors asserted that they were "specialists in theory." Among these, Messrs. Gottl and Oppenheimer were megalomaniacal monomaniacs; Diehl was a narrow-minded ignoramus; and Spiethoff was a man who never was able to publish a book.

In those years the presidency of the Association for Social Policy was held by Professor Eckart, an amiable Rhinelander who, except for a few contributions to the history of German domestic maritime commerce, produced nothing of significance. His competitor was Bernhard Harms, who had popularized the term, "world economy," in Germany. As he had a craving to preside over an association, he founded the "List Society."

My acquaintance with these men made me realize that the German people were no longer salvable. For these characterless simpletons were the select best of the elite of society. At the universities they taught in a field that was the most important one for political education. The masses of the people and the educated classes treated them with highest respect as the intellectual aristocrats in the sciences. What was to become of the youth that had such teachers?

In 1918, in Vienna, Max Weber told me: "You do not like the Association for Social Policy; I like it even less. But it is a fact that it is the only Association of men in our discipline. It is useless for us to criticize it from the outside. We must work with the Association and remove its shortcomings. I am trying it in my way, and you must do it in your way." I followed Weber's advice, but I knew that it would be in vain. As an Austrian, as a *Privatdozent* without a chair, as a "theorist," I always was an outsider in the Association. I was treated with the utmost courtesy, but the other members always looked upon me as an alien.

Max Weber, too, could not have changed the situation. The early death of this genius was a serious blow for Germany. If Weber had lived longer, the German nation could today point to the example of this "Aryan" whom Nazism could not bend. But even this great mind could not have deflected destiny.

In both of these German associations I also met men whose company enriched me greatly. I am remembering especially Max Scheler, the philosopher and sociologist. There were Leopold von Wiese, the sociologist from Cologne, Albert Hahn from Frankfurt, and Moriz Bonn. In 1926, at the Vienna Convention of the German Association for Sociology, I met Walter Sulzbach and his wife, Maria Sulzbach-

Fuerth, and we became the closest of friends. And I should like to mention others, such as Wilhelm Röpke, Alexander Rüstow, Goetz Briefs, Georg Halm, and Richard Passow. The ingenious historian, Eberhard Gothein, and the brilliant, upright Ludwig Pohle unfortunately have already passed away [i.e., before 1940].

Twice there was talk of an appointment for me to a German university. In 1925 it was at the University of Kiel; in 1928 (or was it 1927?) it was at the School of Commerce in Berlin. In both instances the étatists and socialists engaged in passionate agitation against me, and in neither case did the appointment materialize. I did not expect it to turn out otherwise. I was ill-suited to teach the Royal Prussian Police-Science.

XI

Further Inquiries Into Indirect Exchange

In *The Theory of Money and Credit* various treatments of the subjects had not satisfied me. I felt it necessary to remove these deficiencies.

Neither the criticism which my book had aroused, nor the books by other authors published on the problems of indirect exchange* since 1911, could in any way shake my thesis. I owe a great deal to the stimulation of the works of B. M. Anderson, T. E. Gregory, D. H. Robertson, Albert Hahn, Friedrich von Hayek and Fritz Machlup. They induced me to reconsider my theory and improve its presentation. But even where they opposed my reasoning, they confirmed rather than rejected the gist of my theory. I learned genuinely from the writings of these men, and above all, they gave me comfort that I was not alone as an economist and did not work just for the libraries.

As for the rest, the publications on the problems of money and credit of the latest thirty years [1910–1940] were rather unimportant. The decline of scientific thought was shocking. We may say that some works of this period were generally acceptable, albeit some details appeared to be untenable and the presentation was inferior. By and large, the majority of books and essays was worthless.

This harsh judgment is directed especially at those works that purport to show "fallacies" which "orthodox" theory is unable to explain or which directly contradicts it. The authors look upon these fallacies as new and unprecedented because their knowledge of the history of money and banking is defective. They are unable to explain the facts, using "orthodox" theory, because they do not know the theory and cannot think theoretically.

In my belief, it is an important task day by day to peruse the literature

---

* Exchange involving the use of money, as distinguished from direct exchange without the use of money, as barter.

on economic problems and oppose immediately with thorough criticism every absurd and unimportant assertion. Surely, this would not prevent the repetition of old errors, but it would greatly serve the public that is interested in economic questions. Frequently I have discussed the launching of such a journal with friends, but it was impossible to find someone who would publish it without having the assurance of substantial financial subsidy.

Incidentally, I am of the opinion that the refutation of current errors is excellent subject matter to be dealt with in doctor's theses by the young disciples of our science. In fact, the primary requirement of an economist is that he be able to recognize fallacies and refute them critically. Upon occasion I have invited such theses. One which I would like to mention here, because the difficult conditions in Austria in 1920 prevented its publication, is the thesis that earned Helene Lieser the first doctor's degree in the social sciences ever conferred on a woman by an Austrian university. The dissertation dealt with the currency reform programs that were advanced in Austria during the years of the bank-note depreciation. She demonstrated that most of the reform proposals made in European countries around 1920 were not so new as their authors represented them to be.

In my seminar discussions I seized every opportunity to refute popular fallacies. I rather regret that I spent my literary efforts on one more refutation of fallacies that had been exploded a hundred times before. I regret that I spent too much of my limited strength on the fight against pseudo-economics. In hours of quiet reflection, I reaffirmed my resolve to be guided by the passage of Spinoza: *Veritas norma sui et falsi est* ("Let truth be your standard and itself thereby oppose error"). But time and again my temper led me to get involved.

During the inflation I published several essays that were to explain (1) the nature of monetary depreciation and (2) refute the balance-of-payment theory of exchange rates. In addition to the essay on the quantity theory mentioned in the foregoing,* I wrote *"Zahlungsbilanz und Devisenkurse"* ("Balance of Payment and [Foreign] Exchange Rates"†) for the *Mitteilungen des Vereins Österreichischer Banken und Bankiers*

---

* Reference is to item number (1) in preceding sentence.

† Excerpt entitled, "Balance of Payments and Foreign Exchange Rates," to be included in proposed collection, *Ludwig von Mises, On the Manipulation of Money and Credit*; translation by Bettina Bien Greaves, edited by Percy L. Greaves, Jr.

(Reports of the Association of Austrian Banks and Bankers*) which had become a journal available to the public. For the *Schriften des Vereins für Sozialpolitik* (Reports of the Association for Social Policy*) I wrote *"Geldtheoretische Seite des Stabilisierungsproblems"* ("The Stabilization of the Monetary Unit from the Viewpoint of Theory"†). The Association Committee held the essay in abeyance for several months, because its members considered it questionable for me to reject the official thesis that the depreciation of the [German] Mark was caused by reparation payments and French occupation. The essay finally appeared in the summer of 1923 as my second contribution to the journal. In 1919 I had contributed, to a volume on annexation problems, an essay on "The Re-entry of German Austria into the German Empire and the Currency Problem."

In the second edition of my *The Theory of Money and Credit* and in the booklet, *Geldwertstabilisierung und Konjunkturpolitik* ("Monetary Stabilization and Cyclical Policy"‡), I had presented my trade cycle theory in such a way that it completely explained the cycle. The boom is facilitated by credit expansion. But what causes the credit expansion? In the first edition I had not answered this question. Since then I had found the answer. The banks seek to lower the interest rate through credit expansion; monetary policy aiming at "cheap money," and believing that credit expansion is a suitable method for attaining the goal of interest reduction, encourages credit expansion, and endeavors to create the necessary institutional conditions.

The preparation of my *Nationalökonomie* [the German-language predecessor of *Human Action*] afforded me another opportunity to reason through my theory of money and credit, and state it in a new form.[1]

In my book on money I had leveled my criticism at the commonly used concept of "direct exchange without use of money" only inasmuch as it was necessary to reject the doctrine of the neutrality of money. I had dealt with the problems of monetary calculation only as

---

* Title translation only; not available in English.
† English translation to be included in proposed collection of *Ludwig von Mises, On the Manipulation of Money and Credit*.
‡ English translation to be included in proposed collection of *Ludwig von Mises, On the Manipulation of Money and Credit*.
1. *Nationalökonomie: Theorie des Handelns und Wirtschaftens* (Geneva, Switzerland, 1940). This book has not been translated into English. However, after migrating to the United States, Mises rewrote this treatise for an American audience: *Human Action: An Economic Treatise* (Yale University Press, 1949; Liberty Fund, 2007).

it was necessary for my inquiry into the social consequences of monetary depreciation. All else had to be left to the theory of direct exchange. But the basic thought already appeared in the book on money: there are values and valuations, but no measurements of value and no value calculations; the market economy calculates with money prices. This was not new; it was merely a logical conclusion from the theory of subjective value. Hermann Heinrich Gossen had already indicated the conclusion that could be drawn from this for the theory of a socialist economy. The Dutch economist, Nicolaas Gerard Pierson (1839–1909), banker, author, and member of the Dutch parliament, with whose work I became familiar many years later in Hayek's translation, had repeated Gossen's thought.

When I set out to work further on the ideas in my book, *Socialism*, I felt compelled to develop especially the fundamentals of catallactics [namely, ideas not restricted to direct exchange but pertaining to indirect exchange, that is, with the use of money]. Any theory of socialism [involving indirect exchange] that does not have at its very foundation a consideration of the problem of economic calculation, is simply absurd. Therefore, in 1919, I wrote and presented to the *Nationalökonomische Gesellschaft* (Economic Society) the essay, "*Die Wirtschaftsrechnung im sozialistischen Gemeinwesen,*" ("Economic Calculation in the Socialist Commonwealth"). At the suggestion of friends, I published it in the following year in *Archiv für Sozialwissenschaft und Sozialpolitik* (Archives for Social Sciences and Politics). Many of the ideas were later incorporated essentially unchanged in my book, *Gemeinwirtschaft (Socialism)*. The original essay was republished in *Collectivist Economic Planning* in 1935, edited by Friedrich A. von Hayek, under the English title mentioned in the foregoing, "Economic Calculation in the Socialist Commonwealth."

All attempts at disproving the cogency of my thesis were destined to fail because they did not delve into the value-theoretical center of the problem. All these books, theses, and essays endeavored to rescue socialism; they indicated that it was possible nevertheless to construct a socialist system that could calculate economically. They failed to see the very first challenge: How can economic action that always consists of preferring and setting aside, that is, of making unequal valuations, be transformed into equal valuations, and the use of equations? Thus the advocates of socialism came up with the absurd recommendation of substituting equations of mathematical catallactics, depicting an image from which human action is eliminated, for the monetary calculation in the market economy.

My *Nationalökonomie* finally afforded me the opportunity to present the problems of economic calculation in their full significance. Meanwhile, I had to content myself with demonstrating fallacies and contradictions of the proposals for socialist economic calculation. Only in the explanations offered in the third part of my *Nationalökonomie* did my theory of money achieve completion [1940]. Thus I accomplished the project that had presented itself to me thirty-five years earlier. I had merged the theory of indirect exchange with that of direct exchange into a coherent system of human action.

XII

Systems of Social Cooperation

The doctrine of the impossibility of economic calculation in a socialist community constitutes the gist of my book, *Gemeinwirtschaft*, the first edition of which appeared in 1922.[1] In 1927 I published *Liberalismus*,[2] and in 1929, under the title *Kritik des Interventionismus** (*Critique of Interventionism*) I collected various essays on related subjects. Altogether these books offer a comprehensive analysis of the problems of social cooperation. They investigate all conceivable systems of cooperation and examine their feasibility. These studies found their completion in my *Nationalökonomie* [a German antecedent to *Human Action*].[3]

I had intended to include another essay in the collection, *Kritik des Interventionismus*, namely, the essay on "The Nationalization of Credit,"† which had appeared in the *Zeitschrift für Nationalökonomie* in 1929. But the *Zeitschrift's* editors had misplaced the essay, and rediscovered it only after my collection of essays had come off the press. I hold the theories presented in these books to be irrefutable.

In my analysis of these problems I introduced a new point of view, the only one that allows a scientific discussion of these political ques-

---

* Republished in German in 1976 by Wissenschaftliche Buchgesellschaft, Darmstadt, Germany, with a foreword by F. A. Hayek. English translation by Hans F. Sennholz (of the 1929 German edition) entitled *Critique of Interventionism*, published by Arlington House, New Rochelle, N.Y., 1977 [and Foundation for Economic Education, Irvington-on-Hudson, N.Y., 1996].

† Included in *Essays in European Economic Thought*, translated by Louise Sommer (D. Van Nostrand, 1960); this Mises essay now incorporated in Hans F. Sennholz's translation of *Kritik des Interventionismus* [*Critique of Interventionism*].

1. English translation, *Socialism* (Jonathan Cape, 1936; U.S. editions, Macmillan, 1936; Yale University Press, 1951; Liberty Fund, 1981).

2. English translation, *The Free and Prosperous Commonwealth* (Van Nostrand, 1962); *Liberalism: The Classical Tradition* (Liberty Fund, 2005).

3. Published in 1940, just as Mises was departing Switzerland to migrate to the United States, Éditions Union; no English translation available. Reprinted in German, 1980, 2002.

tions. I inquired into the effectiveness of the chosen means to attain the avowed ends, that is, whether the objectives which the recommended measures were to attain would actually be achieved by the means recommended and employed. I demonstrated that an evaluation of the various systems of social cooperation is rather pointless when conducted from an arbitrary point of view. Instead, what only is significant is to judge what the systems indeed accomplish. [Contrarily], all pronouncements from the point of view of a religion, or the different systems of situational ethics, anthropology, positive law and natural law—if disassociated from an evaluation of their effectiveness to attain the desired ends—merely constitute expressions of subjective value judgments.

It is something altogether different to assert that the evolution of the system of private property in the means of production inevitably leads to socialism or interventionism. Even if that were true, it would not disprove my thesis. Neither socialism nor interventionism can acquire meaning and purpose from the alleged but unsupported assertion that history inevitably leads to them. If the "return to capitalism" is really out of the question, as is maintained by socialists and communists, then the fate of our civilization is sealed. But I demonstrated that the doctrine of the inevitability of socialism and interventionism is untenable. Capitalism does not destroy itself. Men wish to abolish it because they expect greater benefits from socialism or interventionism.

Occasionally I entertained the hope that my writings would bear practical fruit and show the way for policy. Constantly I have been looking for evidence of a change in ideology. But I have never allowed myself to be deceived. I have come to realize that my theories explain the degeneration of a great civilization; they do not prevent it. I set out to be a reformer, but only became the historian of decline.

In my publications on social cooperation I have spent much time and effort in dispute against socialists and interventionists of all varieties and trends. My objective, namely, the discrediting of contrary-to-purpose reform proposals, necessitated this effort.

It has been objected that I failed to consider the psychological aspect of the organization problem—that man has a soul, that this soul is said to be uncomfortable in a capitalist system, and also that there is willingness to suffer reduction in living standards in exchange for a more satisfactory labor and employment structure for society.

It is important, first, to determine whether this argument—let us call it the "heart [or emotional] argument"—is incongruent with the original argument [the ability to attain avowed ends] which we may call the "head [or intellectual] argument," still being promoted by socialists and interventionists. The latter socialist argument endeavors to justify its programs with the assertion that capitalism reduces the full development of productive capabilities; production is less than the potential. Socialist production methods are expected to increase output immeasurably, and thereby create the conditions necessary for plentiful provision for everybody. Marxism is completely founded on this head argument. Before Lenin, the Marxists never mentioned that the transition to socialism would lower the standard of living of the masses during the transition period. The Marxists announced immediate improvement in the material situation of the masses, even if occasionally they added that the full blessings of socialist production methods would be reaped only in the course of time. But because of criticism leveled at socialist programs—that they fall far short of promises—the socialists have felt compelled to use the heart argument as an additional reason for adopting socialism.

To judge the heart argument, it is of course important to inquire into the extent of the reduction in economic well-being brought about by adopting a socialist production system. Since this loss cannot be ascertained objectively and measured precisely, the argument between the adherents and opponents of socialism is said to be scientifically insoluble. Economics is said to be unable to settle the dispute.

However, I dealt with this problem in a way that discredits the use of the heart argument. If the socialist system leads to chaos because economic calculation is impossible, and if interventionism cannot attain the objectives proclaimed by its advocates, then it is pure trifling to arrive at these illogical systems via the heart argument. I have never denied that emotional arguments explain the popularity of anti-capitalist policies. But unsuitable proposals and measures cannot be made suitable by such psychic nonsense. If it is true that men cannot tolerate capitalism for psychological ("*seelisch*") reasons, then of course capitalism will fail.

I have been reproached that I have overrated the role of logic and reason in life. According to my critics, there is in *theory* an either/or. Life actually, they insist, requires compromises. What appears in scientific analyses to be irreconcilable is transformed in real life into an acceptable situation. Politics, they say, will find a way of blending conflicting principles. The solution may be called illogical, irrational, and senseless, but it can be fruitful. And this alone matters.

These critics are mistaken. Men wish to carry through that which they deem suitable. To them nothing is more remote than half a realization of a desire. No appeal to historical experience can alter this fact. It is true, those religions that call for some turning away from worldly matters have been compatible with this world. But the rigorous doctrines of Christianity and Buddhism have not really ruled men. That portion of strict dogma which entered popular faith did not stand in the way of activity in life on earth. Real fulfillment of religious commandments was left to monks. Even the princes of the church during the Middle Ages did not allow their actions to be controlled by the commandments of the Sermon on the Mount and other evangelical requirements. The small group of those who took Christianity or Buddhism seriously retreated from worldly affairs. The life of the others was no compromise; it was simply un-Christian and un-Buddhist.

Today we face a problem of a different kind. The masses of people are socialistic or interventionistic; or, at least, anti-capitalistic. The individual does not mean to save his soul from the world; instead he wishes to revolutionize the world. And he wants to see it through. The masses are inflexible in their determination; they would rather destroy the world than yield one iota of their programs.

No consolation can be found in the thought that there always has been interventionism in the pre-capitalistic past. Then far fewer people lived on this earth, and the masses were content with living conditions they would not tolerate today. From capitalism we cannot simply return to some century in the remote past.

XIII

Epistemological Studies

On the ruins of the old religious faith, various sects became established during the course of the nineteenth century, which sought to offer their followers a "substitute" for the lost faith. The most durable of these sects is Positivism,* which is, as Huxley called it (*Collected Essays*, Volume V, page 225), "the incongruous insistence of bad science and eviscerated papistry." In Catholic countries, Positivism, as a reaction against church practices, found many ardent disciples. In Vienna, the city of Holy Clemens Maria Hofbauer, people believed they were really free and unprejudiced if they were Positivists.

Positivism usually is credited with having brought forth sociology. It is true that Auguste Comte coined the term "sociology." But that which is pursued under the name of sociology, excepting when it is just idle talk, has nothing to do with the [alleged] Positivist program of a science of human (social) action that is built on experience, using the methods of Newtonian physics. Such sociology is ethnography, cultural history, and psychology, and uses the old methods of history. Comte did not care about the science of human action which had its beginning with classical economics. And in this his disciples remained faithful to the master.

For some time the German universities rejected Positivism and barred sociology. This hostility had little to do with scientific deliberation; it was of a political nature. When Positivism began to attain success, the German sciences had already assumed their hostile position toward Western thought. They rejected Positivism because it came from France. But their attitude toward the central point of Positivism was rather irresolute. It is remarkable that the historicism of the

---

* On Positivism, see appendix at end of this chapter.

Schmoller School held to the belief that the laws of economics were to be derived from experiences in recorded economic history.*

Actually, the last great contribution of German epistemology was made when dealing with problems that admittedly were not raised by Positivism, but were made controversial by it. The foundation of the theory of scientific understanding of the social sciences had been laid by scholars who wrote before Comte, or did not know him. But the further development of the social sciences was a reaction against Positivism, and no less against the historical materialism of the Marxists.

When I entered the university I saw no possibility of an economic science. Economic history, I was convinced, must use the means and methods of the historical disciplines and can never yield economic laws. And besides economic history there was nothing in economic life, so I believed, that could be made the object of scientific analysis. At the beginning of my university career, there was no more consistent follower of historicism than I!

This structure of my epistemology suffered an irreparable breach when I really learned to know economics. I was perplexed. The writings of the *Methodenstreit*—even Menger's splendid work—did not satisfy me. I was even more disappointed with John Stuart Mill. It was not until many years later that I became acquainted with the work of Cairnes and Senior.

I sought consolation in the thought that it matters above all to advance in science and that the problems of methodology are of lesser importance. But I soon realized the fallacy of this stance. With every problem, the economist faces the basic questions: "From whence do these principles come," "What is their significance," "How do they relate to experience and 'reality'"? These are not problems of method or even research technique; they are themselves the basic questions. Can a deductive system be built without raising the question on what to build?

I searched in vain for an answer in the writings of the Lausanne and Anglo-Saxon Schools. I found the same uncertainty and wavering between irreconcilable opinions. It was not surprising, therefore, that this condition had to lead to a decline of economic thought. Institutionalism [in the United States], on the one hand, and the empty dogmatics of the mathematical schools, on the other hand, are the consequences of this situation.

---

* See chapter 1 for earliest reference in this book to Schmoller.

For a long time I hesitated to present my investigations into epistemological problems to the public because I was aware that they went far beyond the field of economics. In fact, we are dealing here with the opening of a new field of epistemology and logic.

Until now, logic and epistemology only dealt with the experiences of natural sciences and with the deductive system of mathematics. To them, history simply was "no science." Economics at first was not considered a science at all. When it finally had to be included, one simply asserted that economics is the doctrine of the economic aspects of human action. Obviously, this doctrine of *homo oeconomicus* is wholly inapplicable to the subjective value theory. And it does not solve the question of the source of this knowledge of "purely economic" behavior.

Significant progress was achieved when the characteristics of historical methods were recognized and the theories of "understanding" and of "ideal types" were developed. The fact that some disreputable metaphysicians sought refuge with these new theories does not detract from the value of their discovery: no architect can be blamed for the behavior of those who settle in the house he built. But it was rather portentous that a man of Max Weber's caliber also sought to elucidate economic principles by means of his category of "ideal types."

I developed my own theory in a number of critical essays, the first of which was published in 1928. In 1933, these essays were collected and published under the title, *Grundprobleme der Nationalökonomie* (English edition: *Epistemological Problems of Economics*, translated by George Reisman, Princeton, New Jersey; D. Van Nostrand Co., 1960). This collection also contained a new essay on the task and scope of epistemology. In my *Nationalökonomie* I again summarized all this research.

In the essay first published in 1928, I sought to eliminate the distinction between economic and noneconomic action.[1] The subjective value theory had basically removed this spectre. But Menger and Böhm-Bawerk failed to draw all the conclusions that had to be drawn from their basic position.

The next essay, under the title, "Sociology and History," dealt with an investigation of the theoretical science of human action and with history. In this connection I made the mistake of using the term, "sociology," to designate the theory of human action; I should have used the term, "praxeology." That which today is generally called "sociol-

---

1. See above, p. 40, second Author's Note.

ogy" is not theoretical, but historical knowledge. Max Weber was quite right when he defined what he understood to be sociology as cultural science or fine arts. And this sociology, according to Weber, is working with "ideal types." He was mistaken when he assigned also many prax-eological elements to this sociology, and that he saw in economics a science that is working with the intellectual methods of "understand-ing." My essay was directed especially against Max Weber's epistemol-ogy, against which I raised two objections: (1) its failure to comprehend the epistemological characteristics of economics; and (2) its distinction between rational action and actions of other kinds.

In my third essay I contrasted the concept of "understanding" of the historical disciplines with that of "comprehending" of praxeology and economics. And in the essay that introduces the volume, *Grundprob-leme der Nationalökonomie*, I demonstrated the a priori nature of prax-eological knowledge. I had thus drawn the appropriate praxeological conclusion from the scientific development that began during the eigh-teenth century with the discovery of regularity in market phenomena.

I was fully aware that at first my theory would meet with rejection. I knew the Positivist bias of my contemporaries rather well. The ruling panphysicalism is blind to the basic problems of epistemology. Already it looks upon biological problems as "disruptions" of its world view. To these fanatics everything else is nonsensical metaphysics playing with illusory problems. The excesses of this Neopositivism must not be excused, nor even regarded as "beneficial" reaction to the no-less-regrettable fabrications of idealistic philosophy. Surely it is the task of the historian of doctrines to "understand" error and thereby explain it. But "understanding" cannot answer error in its fight against a more satisfactory explanation. I believe I "understand" Positivism historically, but this has nothing to do with the question of whether or not its answers are useful.

I am fully aware that it is impossible to jolt, or better yet, deal a fatal blow to the popularity of Positivist metaphysics with an explanation of the epistemological characteristics of the science of human action. Economic problems are much too complicated to be understood by the people in the same way physics and biology are accepted in general education. Positivism has made classical physics palatable to the peo-ple, and Neopositivism does the same for the present state of physical knowledge. Both misrepresent and oversimplify; not unlike the way the cliché "Man is descended from apes" has misrepresented and oversimplified Darwinism for everyday usage. Much time will pass until man dispenses with such raw simplifications. Until then, there will always be a popular philosophy for use by the common man.

It is another question whether the small number of thinkers will be satisfied with the system of empiricism. I shall not dwell here on the criticism that empiricism simply refuses to acknowledge the science of human action and therefore, contrary to its own emphatically asserted principle, rejects reality because it does not fit into its system. But I should like to raise the question: Is that which Positivism asserts about logical principles really adequate in the long run?

We may call the principles of logic "arbitrarily chosen conventions" that have proven to be practical or useful. But this would merely shift the problem without bringing it any closer to solution. It may be said that man has tried various arbitrarily chosen rules and finally held on to those that proved to be effective. But for what purposes did these rules appear to be effective? If this question is raised, we again face the problems of intellectual comprehension of the things of the world and the problems of explaining and of truth. Therefore, it is futile to attempt to solve the problem of truth with an appeal to usefulness.

May we call these principles of logic "arbitrarily chosen" so that we may choose additional principles that are equally useful for the "purpose"? Surely not! The basic relations which logic uses to connect assertions are necessary and inescapable to human thought. They are so in the sense that basic relations that are irreconcilable are inconceivable. The category of negation is not arbitrarily chosen; it is necessary for human thought. In fact, there is no thought that could do without it. But even if we were to assume that the distinction between "yes" and "no" was won from experience, or that once arbitrarily made it proved itself in experience, we have not yet refuted the contention that before all thought there must be the ability to distinguish between "yes" and "no."

The basic assumptions of logic have been called "rules of the game." But we must then add that this game is our life, that we are born in this game, and that we must play it as long as we live. And for us humans there is no second game that could observe other rules.

Praxeology especially is capable of revealing the fallacies of conventional doctrine because it does not acknowledge a superstitious trust in the word, "purpose." The purpose of action is the attainment of a result in this world, which world is our environment. Therefore, it is purposeful at any rate to adjust to the conditions of this world and its order. If the human mind can give birth to rules of the game that are useful for this adjustment, then only two explanations are feasible: either our minds contain something that belongs to this environment and permits us to understand the environment, that is, an a priori; or environment plies our minds with the rules that permit us to cope with it. In no case is there room for arbitrariness and convention. Logic in us is either effective or affected. It either affects the world through us, or the world affects us through it. It is given to the world, to reality, to life.

It is not at all clear what the obstinate denial of the a priori is to achieve. In order to comprehend the category of means and objective, the question arises: What is it in us that makes it possible to experience certain experiences that reject other outcomes as quite absurd? What sense does it make to assert that we gained this category by experience if we do not know to what other results other experiences could have led? When I say that experience has revealed that A is red, it receives meaning from the fact that our minds can comprehend also other colors. But when it is said that experience has led us to the category of negation or to the category of means and objective, it is an absurd statement. For what could other experience have taught us?

The same is true of conventionalism. What other rules of the game could take the place of logical principles or the praxeological concept of action? Surely, chess could be played in such a way that one of its rules is replaced by any other rule. But can we "play" with thought that does not distinguish between "yes" and "no"? If this question is answered in the negative, it becomes clear that this distinction differs from that of rules of the game. And again we are encountering the inescapable a priori.

When it is asserted that economics is a deductive system that is derived from an a priori point of departure, we do not sketch a plan for a new economics. We merely demonstrate what today's economics is all about.

Of course, it did not escape me that attempts are being made to conduct economics as an experimental science. There is an economics association that adopted as its motto the tenet, "Science is measurement." With Carl Menger, I shall be happy with this movement, which is richly endowed with financial support, to run its full course.* But it

* See page 25.

is not worthwhile to refute again the notion that measurements in the sphere of human action can be made in the same way they are made in physics. Economic statistics is a method of economic history; theoretical insight cannot be won from it.

In economic history too we must understand where "comprehension" becomes inadequate. When all data have been gathered that affected (or could have affected) an event that is to be researched, then only "understanding" can deal with the question of whether and to what extent the various factors contributed to the result. Precisely in this quantitative field, which in the sphere of physics permits "exactness," or at least approximate exactness, lies the task of "understanding" in the sphere of human action. Here there are no constant relations between quantities.

Mathematics and physics are undergoing a severe crisis from which they will emerge in a new form. Little has remained of the cheerful confidence, the indubitable certainty, clarity, and exactness of its tenets, which made them look down with pity on the poor arts and ignore economics entirely. Mathematicians and physicists are beginning— rather belatedly—to perceive logical and epistemological problems. Logic and the epistemology of the sciences of human action cannot learn anything from physics and mathematics. But the "exact" sciences have a great deal to learn from their once-disdained sisters. The gap between the natural sciences and those of human action will not be bridged thereby. A "united" science will emerge only when the physical and chemical processes of physiology that generate the thought, "two times two is four," can be distinguished from those that generate the thought, "two times two is five."

My epistemological studies served the development of logic and epistemology of the sciences of human action, as well as the disclosure of the errors of Positivism, irrationalism, and historicism. And I also sought to cope with polylogism.

APPENDIX (1978): Positivism

As readers who are not oriented by extensive knowledge in the social sciences may have difficulty with terms used by Mises (such as, étatism, historicism, interventionism, in earlier sections of this book), it is equally necessary to make a special effort to understand what Mises

means by Positivism. (This publisher's policy is to use Mises's definitions, in his own words, quoting from one or more of his other books.
That is done in what follows.)

Mises was an anti-Positivist which this anecdote will reveal. A relative had died. An acquaintance was expressing condolence. Mises
closed the matter with the words, "He was a Positivist."

None can really be sure he has understood Mises unless he understands the reasons why Mises was an unalterable anti-Positivist. If the
reader has access to Mises's *The Ultimate Foundation of Economic
Science* (D. Van Nostrand Company, Inc., Princeton, New Jersey,
1962), he should read (or re-read) (1) the Preface, (2) the following
section with the title, "Some Preliminary Observations Concerning
Praxeology Instead of an Introduction," and (3) also Chapter 1 with the
title, "The Human Mind." (Really, the whole book should be read.)
Whoever does not thoroughly understand what Mises means by Positivism, nor the reasons why Mises was a powerful anti-Positivist, will
radically fail to appreciate Mises as one of the most significant thinkers
in the social sciences. Here is a brief extract from pages 6, 7 and 8:

5. *The Reality of the External World*

From the praxeological point of view it is not possible to question the
real existence of matter, of physical objects and of the external world.
Their reality is revealed by the fact that man is not omnipotent. There
is in the world something that offers resistance to the realization of his
wishes and desires. Any attempt to remove by a mere fiat, what annoys
him and to substitute a state of affairs that suits him better for a state of
affairs that suits him less, is vain. If he wants to succeed, he must proceed
according to methods that are adjusted to the structure of something
about which perception provides him with some information. We may
define the external world as the totality of all those things and events
that determine the feasibility or unfeasibility, the success or failure, of
human action. . . .

6. *Causality and Teleology*

Action is a category that the natural sciences do not take into account.
The scientist acts in embarking upon his research work, but in the orbit
of natural events of the external world which he explores there is no
such thing as action. There is agitation, there is stimulus and response,
and, whatever some philosophers may object, there is cause and effect.
There is what appears to be an inexorable regularity in the concatenation
and sequence of phenomena. There are constant relations between en-

tities that enable the scientist to establish the process called measurement. But there is nothing that would suggest aiming at ends sought; there is no ascertainable purpose.

The natural sciences are causality research; the sciences of human action are teleological. In establishing this distinction between the two fields of human knowledge, we do not express any opinion concerning the question whether the course of all cosmic events is or is not ultimately determined by a superhuman being's design. The treatment of this great problem transcends the range of man's reason and is outside the domain of any human science. It is in the realm that metaphysics and theology claim for themselves.

The purpose to which the sciences of human action refer is not the plans and ways of God, but the ends sought by acting men in the pursuit of their own designs. The endeavors of the metaphysical discipline commonly called philosophy of history to reveal in the flux of historical events the hidden plans of God or of some mythical agency (as, for instance, in the scheme of Marx, the material productive forces) are not science.

In dealing with a definite historical fact, for instance with the first World War, the historian has to find out the ends sought by the various individuals and groups of individuals who were instrumental in organizing these campaigns or in fighting the aggressors. He has to examine the outcome resulting from the actions of all people involved and compare it with the preceding state of affairs as well as with the intentions of the actors. But it is not the historian's business to search after a "higher" or "deeper" sense that manifested itself in the events or was realized by them. Perhaps there is such a hidden "higher" or "deeper" purpose or significance in the succession of historical events. But for mortal man there is no way open to learn something about such "higher" or "deeper" meanings.

7. The Category of Action

All the elements of the theoretical sciences of human action are already implied in the category of action and have to be made explicit by expounding its contents. As among these elements of teleology is also the category of causality, the category of action is the fundamental category of epistemology, the starting point of any epistemological analysis.

The very category or concept of action comprehends the concepts of means and ends, of preferring and putting aside, viz., of valuing, of success and failure, of profit and loss, of costs. As no action could be devised and ventured upon without definite ideas about the relation of cause and effect, teleology presupposes causality.

Further, read Mises's *Theory and History* (Yale University Press, New Haven, Connecticut, 1957), Chapter 11 entitled, "The Challenge of Scientism," pages 240–263. The first five paragraphs read as follows:

1. *Positivism and Behaviorism*

What differentiates the realm of the natural sciences from that of the sciences of human action is the categorical system resorted to in each in interpreting phenomena and constructing theories. The natural sciences do not know anything about *final causes**; inquiry and theorizing are entirely guided by the category of causality. The field of the sciences of human action is the orbit of purpose and of conscious aiming at ends; it is teleological.

Both categories were resorted to by primitive man and are resorted to today by everybody in daily thinking and acting. The most simple skills and techniques imply knowledge gathered by rudimentary research into causality. Where people did not know how to seek the relation of cause and effect, they looked for a teleological interpretation. They invented deities and devils to whose purposeful action certain phenomena were ascribed. A god emitted lightning and thunder. Another god, angry about some acts of men, killed the offenders by shooting arrows. A witch's evil eye made women barren and cows dry. Such beliefs generated definite methods of action. Conduct pleasing to the deity, offering of sacrifices and prayer were considered suitable means to appease the deity's anger and to avert its revenge; magic rites were employed to neutralize witchcraft. Slowly people came to learn that meteorological events, disease, and the spread of plagues are natural phenomena and that lightning rods and antiseptic agents provide effective protection while magic rites are useless. It was only in the modern era that the natural sciences in all their fields substituted causal research for finalism.

The marvelous achievements of the experimental natural sciences prompted the emergence of a materialistic metaphysical doctrine, positivism. Positivism flatly denies that any field of inquiry is open for teleological research. The experimental methods of the natural sciences are the only appropriate methods for any kind of investigation. They alone are scientific, while the traditional methods of the sciences of human action are metaphysical, that is, in the terminology of positivism, superstitious and spurious. Positivism teaches that the task of science is exclusively the description and interpretation of sensory experience. It

---

* Definition of *final cause*: Purpose; the object or end to be reached by an action or process. Also, *teleology*: The branch of cosmology that treats of final causes (that is, purposes). Also, *finalism*, same as *teleology*.

rejects the introspection of psychology as well as all historical disciplines. It is especially fanatical in its condemnation of economics. Auguste Comte, by no means the founder of positivism but merely the inventor of its name, suggested as a substitute for the traditional methods of dealing with human action a new branch of science, sociology. Sociology should be social physics, shaped according to the epistemological pattern of Newtonian mechanics. The plan was so shallow and impractical that no serious attempt was ever made to realize it. The first generation of Comte's followers turned instead toward what they believed to be biological and organic interpretation of social phenomena. They indulged freely in metaphorical language and quite seriously discussed such problems as what in the social "body" should be classed as "intercellular substance." When the absurdity of this biologism and organicism became obvious, the sociologists completely abandoned the ambitious pretensions of Comte. There was no longer any question of discovering a posteriori laws of social change. Various historical, ethnographical, and psychological studies were put out under the label sociology. Many of these publications were dilettantish and confused; some are acceptable contributions to various fields of historical research. Without any value, on the other hand, were the writings of those who termed sociology their arbitrary metaphysical effusions about the recondite meaning and end of the historical process which had been previously styled philosophy of history. Thus, Emile Durkheim and his school revived under the appellation, group mind, the old specter of romanticism; and the German school of historical jurisprudence, the *Volkgeist*.

In spite of this manifest failure of the positivist program, a neopositivist movement has arisen. It stubbornly repeats all the fallacies of Comte. The same motive inspires these writers that inspired Comte. They are driven by an idiosyncratic abhorrence of the market economy and its political corollary: representative government, freedom of thought, speech, and the press. They long for totalitarianism, dictatorship, and the ruthless oppression of all dissenters, taking, of course, for granted that they themselves or their intimate friends will be vested with the supreme office and the power to silence all opponents. Comte without shame advocated suppression of all doctrines he disliked. The most obtrusive champion of the neopositivist program concerning the sciences of human action was Otto Neurath who, in 1919, was one of the outstanding leaders of the short-lived Soviet regime of Munich and later cooperated briefly in Moscow with the bureaucracy of the Bolsheviks.* Knowing they cannot

* Otto Neurath, "Foundations of the Social Sciences," *International Encyclopedia of Unified Science*, Vol. 2, No. 1.

advance any tenable argument against the economists' critique of their plans, these passionate communists try to discredit economics wholesale on epistemological grounds.

The two main varieties of the neopositivistic assault on economics are panphysicalism and behaviorism. Both claim to substitute a purely causal treatment of human action for the—as they declare unscientific—teleological treatment.

XIV

My Teaching in Geneva

My position with the Chamber of Commerce entitled me to retire after thirty years of service with a lifetime pension of nearly 15,000 schillings per year.[1] Every Chamber official received double credit for two-and-a-half years of war service. In addition, I received credit for three years of pre-war service. And as each service year which was begun was counted as a full year, I could retire on October 1, 1932. I always had anticipated this date with mixed feelings. On the one hand, I was eager to shed the obligations of my office in order to devote myself exclusively to scientific work; on the other hand, I had to admit that the promised pension seemed to be rather precarious considering the general uncertainty of conditions.

The very existence of the Chambers of Commerce had become troublesome to all political parties because of the economic activity I had launched. To the Social Democrats the Chamber had always been a thorn in their eye. The Greater Germans [Pan-Germans] saw in the intellectual ascendency of the Chamber an obstacle to the merger of Austria with Germany. In the Christian Social Party the agrarian wing under Dollfuss' leadership had gained the upper hand; the agrarians considered the Chambers as the archenemy of their policies. All parties planned to eliminate the Chambers in a restructuring of economic society. The cliché, a *Ständestaat* [corporate state], was quite meaningless in Austria; it merely shielded the aspiration of the Christian Social Party and its allied homeguard for complete party rule. No one could say what he actually meant by *Ständestaat*. But everyone knew for certain that the Chamber of Commerce, Handicrafts, and Industry

---

1. It is impossible to calculate with any accuracy the value of Mises's anticipated pension of 15,000 Austrian schillings. However, the 1929 Baedeker quotes the Austrian schilling at US$0.14 which would mean that 15,000 Austrian schillings in 1932 would have amounted to about US$2,100/year in 1932 dollars.

was unsuited for a *Ständestaat*, and that it had to be removed as a "liberal" institution.

The Chambers had only two other officials besides me who were able to come to their defense: Dr. Wilhelm Becker in Vienna and Dr. Wilhelm Taucher in Graz who, as a second occupation, was assistant professor at the University of Graz. In late 1937 and early 1938 Taucher was Secretary of Commerce in Schuschnigg's cabinet. Both took a dim view of my immediate retirement and induced me to take up the cause of the Chambers and the defense of our pension claims. Our personal interests were at stake. The internal struggle for Austria had come to an end as the banking crisis had made the banks, and thereby big industry, directly dependent on the Central Bank.

In the spring of 1934 I received, quite unexpectedly, an invitation to assume the chair for international economic relations at the Institut Universitaire des Hautes Etudes Internationales in Geneva during the academic year 1934–1935. I accepted immediately. I did not formally resign from the Chamber, and retained the direction of the Chamber department for finance, promising to return to Vienna as often as it should become necessary. But I forfeited two-thirds of my salary during this absence.

When I moved to Geneva in the fall of 1934, I had to assume that my appointment was for one year only. But my contract was renewed and I stayed in Geneva until the end of the academic year, 1939–1940.

For me it was a liberation to be removed from the political tasks I could not have escaped in Vienna, and from the daily routines in the Chamber. Finally, I could devote myself completely and almost exclusively to scientific problems.

The Institut was the achievement of its directors, William E. Rappard and Paul Mantoux. The teaching obligations of its instructors were minor: one hour of lecture and two hours of seminar per week. There was a friendly atmosphere between teachers and students, and the spirit of genuine liberalism flourished in this unique institution. All around us the barbarian flood was rising and we all knew we were fighting with nothing but forlorn hope.

The Geneva of those years will be remembered in history as the seat of the League of Nations. The League was never "real." Out of a great idea the diplomats had made an office with several hundred employees. There were officials who had no interest other than to preserve their positions. At the head of this bureaucracy stood an unimaginative, narrow-minded French bureaucrat, Monsieur Avenol. The officials were similar to their chief.

But the League of Nations did not fail on account of the inability and indolence of its officials. It never came to life because it lacked the ideological foundation. In a liberal world, the individual states and nations can cooperate peacefully without a super-national organization. In a world animated by nationalism, conflicts can be removed neither by treaties nor the establishment of international offices.

The failure of the League of Nations also paralyzed the development of the Institut of Rappard and Mantoux. The young people who attended it came to Geneva not just to attend the lectures and seminars. In Geneva they sought to escape from the narrow nationalism of their own countries and grasp at the spirit of international cooperation. But what they saw of the League of Nations dismayed them and deprived them of their courage. They found the Geneva atmosphere unbearable. As much as they approved of the Institut, they were disappointed by everything they learned about "international life."

The outbreak of World War II greatly limited the activity of the Institut. Now its students were Swiss citizens only, and political refugees who were waiting for an opportunity to emigrate to America. In July 1940, I left the Institut because I could no longer face living in a country that considered my presence a political liability and a danger to its security.

XV

The Struggle for Austria's Survival

When I moved to Geneva I did not deceive myself about the obvious hopelessness of the fight for Austria's survival.

The politicians in power lacked the ability to fight this battle against foreign powers; foreign countries were totally alien to them. Those politicians understood neither foreign languages, foreign mentality, nor foreign political beliefs. They were even incapable of informing the foreign diplomats and journalists located in Vienna. The diplomats researched the pleasures of living high in Vienna, and enjoyed winter sports in the Alps. Business affairs were handled by the press counsellors of the several missions; most active among them was the Italian, Eugenio Morreale.

The Austrian government did not at all concern itself with foreign newspapermen; informing the latter was left to the Social Democrats.

The total incapability of the Social Democratic leaders had catastrophic effects. In 1918 Otto Bauer had elevated the demand for unification with Germany to a plank in the Social Democratic Party platform. His starting point was the thought that in highly industrialized Germany the rule of the proletariat was permanently assured. But in Austria, in which the majority of the population consisted of farmers, farm workers, and craftsmen, he feared a defeat of the proletariat by the other classes. Even when the National Socialists [Nazis] seized power in Germany, Bauer refused to alter his policy. In his stubbornness he failed to see that his adherence to the German-Austrian unification program was grist in the mill of the Nazis.

The Social Democrats simply refused to understand that Italy was the only government ready to support Austria in her fight against a Nazi take-over. They fought passionately against a "fascist course" for foreign policy. In January 1934, Dollfuss was ready to surrender to the National Socialists [Nazis]. The negotiations had progressed rather far when, at the latest moment, Italy put in its veto against Austrian annexation. Mussolini sent his Under-Secretary of State, Suvich, to Vienna to assure the government of his support. The Social Democrats then acted with a crowning touch of stupidity. Their journal, *The Labor Press*, accused Suvich of having deserted from the Austrian Army in World War I. Social Democrats organized violent street demonstrations against this delegate of Mussolini. Only a massive commitment of the police and the homeguard shielded Under Secretary Suvich from personal injury; to give Suvich some redress, the government then suspended the mailing of *The Labor Press* for one month. The Social Democrats answered with even wilder demonstrations, which resulted in open fighting and in which the organizers were crushed by government troops and the homeguard. This was the end of the rule of the Social Democratic Party in the city government in Vienna.

Leaders of the Social Democratic Party, who had escaped to London, Paris, and Prague, now opposed any support for Austria in her fight against Hitler. Between the fascism of Austria and that of the Nazis there is no difference, they contended. And it was held that it was not the task of the Western democracies to get embroiled in the struggle between two fascist groups.

The powers, anyway, had no intention of opposing Hitler. From March 1933 the fate of Austria lay entirely in the hands of Italy. If Italy had not been ready to interfere, Hitler, in July 1934, would have intervened in the repression by the Austrian government against rebel Austrian Nazis and German "tourists." When British policies drove Italy, relative to the Ethiopian problem, into the arms of Hitler, the fate of Austria was sealed.

There are no words strong enough to describe the absurdity of British policies between the two wars. The British were not to be swayed. They were convinced that they knew and understood everything better. They distrusted everyone; but they believed everything the Nazis said.

The behavior of the Czechs was even more absurd. Even in 1938 Benes saw the restoration of the Habsburg Monarchy as an evil greater than annexation of Austria by Germany. The sympathy of the French quite openly lay on the side of Hitler; nearly all educated Frenchmen were reading the *Gringoire* which openly defended Hitler. *Quos deus vult perdere, dementat* (Those whom the gods would destroy they first make mad)!

It was absolutely impossible to oppose such stupidity. When I first arrived in Geneva I had hoped to be able to contribute somehow to the enlightenment of leading personalities there. But I soon came to realize that this was a futile undertaking. "We Englishmen," a Labor Party man once told me, "will never again wage war." I asked, "But what will you do if Hitler should attack Great Britain?" His answer was startling: "Then we will be ruled and exploited by German instead of British capitalists; it does not make any difference to the people."

Beginning in 1931 the League of Nations was represented in Vienna by a Dutchman by the name of Rost Van Tonningen. He openly conducted pro-Nazi propaganda while he was in Vienna. My Viennese friends could not believe that I was unable to arrange for Rost's recall from Vienna. (When Van Tonningen later withdrew from the League of Nations' service and returned to Holland, he was immediately appointed Deputy-Führer of the National Socialist [Nazi] Party in The Netherlands.)

Only *one* nation on the European continent attempted seriously to oppose Hitler, namely, the Austrian nation. Only after five years of successful resistance, and deserted by all, did little Austria surrender. The whole world breathed a sigh of relief; now Hitler finally would be satisfied; now he would deal peacefully with other nations!

But twenty-seven months later Hitler was "master" of the European continent!

POSTSCRIPT

Age does not depend upon years, but upon health and attitude. Many men are born old, but some never grow old. Ludwig von Mises was one of those ever-youthful men whose season of hope, enterprise, and energy lasted unto his death on October 10, 1973, at the age of 92. Always active in thought, always eager to ponder new ideas, his mind was ever young. Satisfied, yet ever dissatisfied; settled, yet ever unsettled; seeing clearly, yet ever searching for new horizons.

There were two lives to him—the life of the European economist who valiantly defended European civilization until it had vanished in the darkness of World War II, and the life of the American scholar who was planting fertile seeds for a rebirth of American values and virtues. Each life spanned one generation, altogether some sixty years of discovery, always in advance of his time—as a pioneer for the generation to come.

Professor von Mises penned his *Notes and Recollections* in 1940 as a final restatement of principles that had guided him on his European course. As a refugee on the roads of France, Spain, and Portugal he had observed firsthand many manifestations of the political and economic ideologies that, in final analysis, had created the turmoil and made him a refugee from his beloved Austria. He remembered his numerous encounters with the statist intellectuals who for many decades had espoused and popularized the doctrines of conflict and violence. Europe, in fact the whole world, was now reaping the bitter fruits of the philosophies he had battled all his life.

Ludwig von Mises, Notes and Recollections reads like a last testimony of a resistance fighter who is looking back because there may be no tomorrow. It is a statement of defiance, proud in his efforts, humble in his failures, exalted in his integrity to the end. It is faithful to the Virgil motto Mises chose for his life: *Tu ne cede malis sed contra au-*

dentior ito ("Do not yield to the bad, but always oppose it with courage"). *Ludwig von Mises, Notes and Recollections* is forever hoisting his Austrian banner avowing: Always Walk in Courage.

Ludwig von Mises chose not to leave a manuscript that reminisces of his life in America. It would be idle speculation for us to wonder why, in the late evening of his life, he chose not to record in writing his American experiences. Surely, he could have done so as he remained active and creative well into his 90th year. Instead, he chose to remain silent and made us forever wonder how he appraised the American scene and how he saw himself on that scene. Reminiscing about Europe he had concluded:

> Occasionally I entertained the hope that my writings would bear practical fruit and show the way for policy, and to that end I have constantly searched for evidences of an ideological change [see page 80]. But I have never allowed myself to be deceived. I recognized that my theories merely explain the decline of a great civilization; they did not prevent it. I set out to be a reformer, but only became the historian of decline.

Reminiscing about his thirty productive years in the United States, did he see the dawn of a new day? Or did he conclude once again that he had become the historian of decline?

He left us without answering this most vexing question. Perhaps, in his great wisdom, he did not want to undermine the foundations of our hope which, though it be exceedingly deceitful, is guiding our lives in a more pleasant way and rousing us to stay firm and renew our efforts. He seeks to reach Americans through his prodigious work that has made him the most important economist of the century. But he was more than a great economist with a keen analytical mind. He was the most undaunted and uncompromising champion of economic and political liberty. For more than half a century he was a rallying-point for the forces of freedom, never wavering or compromising, imperturbable and unyielding, unaffected by the scorn and ridicule of his adversaries, or by the temptations of this world. By his writings, Ludwig von Mises has sown the seeds of a regeneration that are bearing fruit the world over.

The United States in 1940

When Ludwig von Mises arrived in the New World, on August 2, 1940, in New York, the same ideological forces he had encountered in Europe were deeply entrenched in the United States. The Great Depression which he had so clearly foreseen was lingering on; it was not liquidated until the impact of massive defense spending substituted production of destructive weapons in place of stagnation and unemployment. Various reform phases of the New Deal were seriously affecting the smooth functioning of the economic order. A wide variety of programs designed to bolster farm income was restricting agricultural activity. Labor was suffering from minimum-wage and maximum-hour legislation, as well as from the restraints of collective bargaining. Depositors and investors were hampered by banking and security laws. Huge federal projects on the Tennessee, Columbia, and Colorado rivers were ushering in federal control over energy. Social Security had launched a vast redistribution program that was to take more and more income from the working population and give it to an increasing number of retired people. In all phases of economic life the New Deal meant greatly expanded government activity and huge federal expenditures.

The New Deal was an early manifestation of the statist ideology that was infecting and inflaming the world. Throughout most of his productive life in Europe, Professor von Mises had encountered more advanced symptoms of this very ideology. With the rapid growth of economic legislation and administrative power had come comprehensive price and wage controls, massive budget deficits and rampant inflation, redistribution of income and wealth through taxation and inflation, consumption of productive capital, and finally, the impairment of social cooperation. The failure of radical interventionism, especially the irreparable harm it does to peaceful division of labor, then gives birth to the final stage—political tyranny in the guise of fascism or communism. Ludwig von Mises was fleeing from this final stage to seek refuge with a society still in its early stage.

In spite of the great tradition of individual freedom and the private property order in the United States, the Great Depression provided the opportunity for statism to advance a giant step. There were too few defenders of the market order, too few spokesmen for freedom who could explain that the monetary follies during the Harding and the Coolidge Administrations had set the stage for the Great Depression, that the Hoover policies of trade restrictions, price manipulations, and tax increases had greatly aggravated the situation, and that the Roosevelt policies of spending, taxing, and regulating had prolonged the interventionist debacle. Instead, the intellectual forces of statism succeeded in placing the blame for the Depression and the great suffering it brought to the American people on the individual enterprise system. The New Deal was made to appear as the new savior from want and fear.

For a time, say 1933 to 1937, President Roosevelt and his economic advisors adhered to the "institutional approach" and shaped economic policies in accordance with the doctrines of Thorstein Veblen, W. C. Mitchell, J. M. Clark, J. R. Commons, and many others. Although Institutional Economics may be essentially an American product, its resemblance to earlier German Historicism was considerable. Both emphasized the importance of social institutions and denied the principles and laws of the market. Both emphasized social change and evolution, and rejected inexorable values and axioms. Both vigorously attacked Classical and Neoclassical economics on grounds of their theoretical abstractions and deductions, and both spurned the Classical and Neoclassical premises of philosophical individualism and the motivation which rests on action determined by preferring what one likes more to what one likes less, whether out of so-called self-interest or for others. The "younger" groups in both schools, German Historicism and American Institutionalism, then sought to establish a "new economics" that afforded the intellectual support for social reform and political control.

The great debate between German Historicism and the Austrian School had opened in 1883 with the publication of Carl Menger's *Untersuchungen über die Methode der Sozialwissenschaften und der Politischen Oekonomie insbesondere* (*Inquiry into the Method of Social Sciences and of Political Economy in Particular*), and closed with the advent of World War II, which forever disproved and shattered the principal tenets of German Historicism. In the United States, the debate between the powerful forces of Institutionalism and the remnants of Neoclassical economics, which had begun with Thorstein Veblen's *Theory of the Leisure Class* (1899), was still in progress. Ludwig von Mises's arrival on the American scene meant urgently needed reinforcement for the remnant, which was led by such eminent scholars as B. M. Anderson, F. A. Fetter, E. W. Kemmerer, Henry Hazlitt, and others.

At the center of scholarly discussion that had been going on in the United States since the late 1930s stood a new theory that embodied some of the oldest errors in the history of economic thought. Lord Keynes' *The General Theory of Employment, Interest, and Money* was conceived during the Depression and born during the perplexities of stagnation and unemployment. It rejected the monetary reasoning of the economists as "Orthodox" or "Neoclassical" and, instead, offered an apparent justification for economic policies that were popular. The "new theory" presented a new vindication of old policies, and noisily placed the blame for the Great Depression on the doorsteps of business and the individual enterprise order. But above all, it popularized the oldest of all economic fallacies, inflationism, as the appropriate means for recovery. Lord Keynes' justification of "deficit spending" explains his unprecedented success with contemporary governments and the political parties in power.

To Ludwig von Mises, Lord Keynes merely revived "the self-contradictory dogmas of the various sects of inflationism." Keynes did not add anything to the armory of inflation, which Mises had battled indefatigably ever since his *The Theory of Money and Credit* was first published in 1912. Long before Keynesianism prescribed government spending and deficit financing as a cure for economic recovery, Mises had encountered similar recipes by German inflationists such as Knapp, Bendixen, Dühring, Lexis, Helfferich, and many others. Again and again he had warned against their doctrines and policies. And when his warnings went unheeded he had watched the inevitable consequences come to pass during the hyperinflations in postwar Europe. In the United States, he was to sound the same warning against similar follies.

During the early 1940s, when Professor von Mises was about to take his place in American economic thought, many writers were focusing on the problems of "social welfare." There were socialist thinkers, such as Abba P. Lerner, Oscar Lange, A. Bergson, and P. M. Sweezy, who were concerned with macro-economic schemes for a more or less managed economy. Their theories of "Welfare Economics" arrived at conclusions that were basically identical with those of the Marxians, although they proceeded via different routes. While Karl Marx had built his structure on the labor theory of value and the exploitation doctrine, the New Welfare economists were constructing their doctrines on the idea of an aggregate optimum of "social utility" in a controlled economy.

In Europe, Professor von Mises had engaged the political forces of Social Democracy, whose language was Marxian and whose program was that of winning political power, taking over the control of the bourgeois state by constitutional electoral means. In the United States, Professor von Mises encountered the Fabian socialists who envisioned an evolutionary socialism by turning the existing state into a "welfare state" through progressive reforms. The Fabians practiced "permeation" by which they hoped to get their ideas adopted by any party or person that would listen to them. They were "gradualist" socialists who welcomed any and all theoretical doctrines that questioned the private property order.

In Europe they called themselves "socialists," which is a term freely used, since the days of Robert Owen, by all those seeking a new way of life based on social control. In the United States many assumed the label of "progressive liberals" while promoting their Fabian programs of economic regulation and political control. As a "classical liberal," Professor von Mises found himself in the awkward position of confrontation with American liberals who evoked an "affirmative liberal state" as their immediate goal. They were speaking the same language, employing identical political and economic terms, and yet, they were worlds apart in political and economic philosophy.

To many American economists, Ludwig von Mises was practically unknown. It is a sorry fact that few American economists can actually read a foreign language. Foreign knowledge becomes available only through translation, which largely depends on the erudition of publishers and their appreciation of foreign works. There is a language barrier that separates the English-speaking world from the rest of mankind. Even Carl Menger's pioneering work of the 1870s and 1880s was unavailable in English and remained untranslated until the 1950s. Some of Böhm-Bawerk's writings had been translated, but his completed works became available in English only in 1959. And Mises's classic, *The Theory of Money and Credit*, first published in 1912, remained untranslated until 1934. By that time it was too late to prevent the economic disaster of the Great Depression. In the enthusiastic reception that was given to the "Keynesian Revolution," his so-called Austrian explanation was simply ignored.

As the language barrier isolated the Anglo-American world from foreign thought, so did the Austrians find themselves isolated against the world through their philosophical and methodological individualism. Their uncompromising rejection of holism and statism, of positivism and scientism, of mathematics and statistics in economic theory, set them apart from the economic fraternity of the 1930s.

There were few Americans who were aware that Professor von Mises, in his *The Theory of Money and Credit,* had offered an explanation of the business cycle phenomena that was completely integrated with general economic theory. He had proved that, contrary to Keynesian policy prescriptions, ever-vigilant government need not check and balance an unstable economic order. In fact, there can be no business cycle of boom and depression if government does not create it. For government alone can and does generate the boom and bust cycle through toleration and protection of inflationary expansion of money and credit. The recession or depression is merely an inevitable readjustment of the production system in which the market liquidates unsound malinvestments.

His monetary work was a milestone in the history of economic knowledge. Written well before World War I, it clearly anticipated the monetary chaos that resulted from the rise of statism in the guise of nationalism and socialism. And it observed so clearly that inflation was the inevitable outcome of the social ideology to which the people were committed. They were lamenting over inflation, but were enthusiastically supporting policies that could not be conducted without inflation.

It was this book that helped me discover the Austrian world of deductive reasoning and theoretical deliberation when I was a young graduate student in postwar Germany. It prompted me a few years later to seek out Professor von Mises and study with him at New York University where he lectured and conducted his seminar.

There were not many American scholars who were acquainted with Mises's *Socialism,* which was revolutionary in its critique of the socialist order. First published in 1922, it was translated only in 1936 when totalitarian socialism was setting about to conquer the world. For the first time in the history of Marxism an economist had revealed the fundamental economic deficiency of socialism: its inability to solve the problem of economic calculation. Without a common denominator for economic calculation, which in the market order is the market price, a socialist society cannot rationally allocate its labor, capital, and other resources, and distribute the yields of production. It is unable to determine whether its production yields a social profit or suffers a loss. It cannot determine the contribution made and the reward earned by each worker. In short, it cannot rationally and economically compare the multiplicity of costs with the returns of production and, therefore, is a chaotic system that suffers from chronic inefficiency and waste. Even the socialists had to acknowledge these Mises objections to the socialist order. In their frantic search for "solutions" they had to acknowledge Professor von Mises as one of Europe's most distinguished economists.

There were even fewer American scholars who were aware of Mises's great philosophical achievements. In 1933 he had published a collection of essays that established the legitimacy of praxeology, the science of universally valid laws of human action. The collection was not to become available in English until 1960 when it was published by D. Van Nostrand under the title of *Epistemological Problems of Economics*. His *Nationalökonomie* which had just been released in Geneva, Switzerland (1940), was built on this very epistemology. In those days probably few copies ever reached the United States.

Mises in America

The way to fame is through much tribulation. Ludwig von Mises's road was no exception. In America, where not only the language barrier but also the ideological chasm had isolated the economics profession from the world of Austrian economics, Mises's great achievements were practically unknown to the general public. This fact alone may explain why American universities did not find a regular academic post for the foremost European exile. From 1945 on, it is true, he was engaged as a Visiting Professor at the Graduate School of Business Administration at New York University, as long as the Volker Fund in Burlingame, California, and other foundations and funds provided his support. But even when they became conversant with his thought during the 1950s and 1960s, they were not prepared to employ a great mind like Mises. The world wants geniuses, but would like them to be just like other people. Mises was the embodiment of methodological and political individualism, which was anathema to American academia.

In seventeen years of effective teaching at the University of Vienna the authorities did not let him go any further in his academic career than as an unsalaried Associate Professor. In twenty-four years of teaching in the United States he served as unsalaried Visiting Professor. Among the many institutions of higher learning in Europe and America, both the University of Vienna and New York University distinguished themselves in that they tolerated his teaching, provided it did not cost them a penny. In Vienna, the University was "permeated by a spirit that was alien to culture and science." At New York University he was surrounded by colleagues to whom the spirit of classical liberalism was alien and irksome. In Vienna, the educational level of graduate students was so low and the educational system so inadequate that few graduates of law, the social sciences, and philosophy were actually prepared for their professions. No more than ten among one hundred Viennese attorneys at law could read a journal in English or French. At New York University the educational level of American students was no higher than that of Austrian students; only a modest percentage could actually read a French or German book. The many hundreds of students who, over the span of twenty-four years, sat through Professor von Mises's classes, in order to earn the necessary graduation credits, were studying accounting and business administration. Few of them really sought economic knowledge and comprehended what it was all about.

To him, young friends meant fresh aspiration to truth and hope for better things. Among the most faithful attendees of his New York University Graduate School of Business Administration seminar, the following are well remembered: Robert G. Anderson, William Burdick, Frank Dierson, Edward Facey, Paul Fair, Richard L. Fruin, Bettina Bien-Greaves, Percy L. Greaves, Jr., Robert Guarnieri, Henry Hazlitt, Ronald Hertz, Isidor Hodes, Wayne Holman, Israel Kirzner, George Koether, Joseph Keckeissen, Robert H. Miller, Toshio Murata, Sylvester Petro, George Reisman, Murray N. Rothbard, Hans F. Sennholz, Mary Homan-Sennholz, Louis Spadaro.

Professor von Mises's main teaching effort in Vienna focused on his non-accredited "private seminar" in which as many as forty to fifty young people gathered around him for informal discussions of important economic and philosophical issues. From this small Mises circle in Vienna emerged some of the most eminent scholars of our day — e.g., Friedrich A. von Hayek, Gottfried von Haberler, Fritz Machlup, Oskar Morgenstern, Erich Voegelin, and others. "There was greatness in this unassuming exchange of ideas," Mises later recalled, "and in it we all found happiness and satisfaction."

In New York Professor von Mises conducted a formal seminar for students interested in writing master's reports and doctoral dissertations. The weekly meetings attracted not only a few serious degree candidates, but also many nonregistered students from the New York

City area. The circle was joined by some of his eminent friends, such as Henry Hazlitt and Lawrence Fertig, and other scholars who happened to be in town. While it may still be too early for an objective verdict on this New York circle of his younger disciples, it may be observed without much contradiction that they not only are ably carrying on the Austrian tradition, but also have since then formed the very nucleus of a growing reformation movement. Their great dedication and staunch loyalty to Misesian ideals, their courage and productivity, have made them an ideological force that is felt throughout the country. Their ranks, in turn, are swelling with ever more of their own students and disciples who are expounding the Mises heritage.

A great man can be held down neither by exile, nor change of environment, language barrier, or any other handicap. Ludwig von Mises had barely settled in New York City when, supported by small foundation grants, he set out to write an explanation of the international conflicts that caused both World Wars. His *Omnipotent Government* (1944) is not only a history of the fall of Germany, but also a powerful critique of the political, social and economic ideologies that have shaped European history in the latest two hundred years.

Until the middle of the nineteenth century, Western man was moving toward the establishment of democracy, the evolution of capitalism, capital formation, and an unprecedented rise in the standard of living. Europe was enjoying an epoch of great artistic and literary achievements, of immortal musicians, painters, writers, and philosophers. The guiding stars of the Germans were Schiller and Goethe, Mozart and Beethoven. But when individualism and liberalism gave way to nationalism and socialism, the peaceful cooperation of nations came to an end. German Nazism was totalitarian socialism. The ordeal of two World Wars was the inevitable result of holistic doctrines and policies that are so popular today. Men want totalitarianism, Mises observed, that is, conditions in which all human affairs are managed by government. They hail every step toward more government as "progress" toward a more perfect world, and adore the state with all its methods of coercion and compulsion, threat and violence. "The responsibility for the present state of world affairs lies with those doctrines and parties that have dominated the course of politics in the latest decades" (ibid., page 12).

In his *Bureaucracy* (Yale University Press, New Haven, Connecticut,

1944), which appeared soon after *Omnipotent Government,* Ludwig von Mises addressed himself to the same basic issue: Should authoritarian socialism be substituted for individualism and democracy? In *Omnipotent Government* he analyzed the problems that characterized the antagonism between German socialism and capitalism. In his *Bureaucracy* he contrasted in systematic fashion the characteristic features of socialist management with profit system management.

It does not make any sense, Mises contended, to complain that bureaucratic management is wasteful, inefficient, slow, and enmeshed in red tape. It is bound to comply with detailed rules and regulations that are issued by the authorities. There is no market price for government services, e.g., protection by the armed forces or police, which can be checked by economic calculation. Therefore, it is a mistake to compare the efficiency of a government department with the operation of a private enterprise that is subject to the restraints of the market.

The essential difference is not efficiency or waste, but one of organization: Should society be organized on the basis of private ownership in the means of production or on the basis of public bureaucratic control? The private property order means individual enterprise and consumer control in all economic matters. The system of public control, on the other hand, means government control of every sphere of economic life and the supremacy of politicians and bureaucrats as planners and production supervisors. The champions of such an order, Mises observed,

> call themselves progressives, but they recommend a system which is characterized by rigid observance of routine and by a resistance to every kind of improvement. They call themselves liberals, but they are intent upon abolishing liberty. They call themselves democrats, but they yearn for dictatorship. They call themselves revolutionaries, but they want to make the government omnipotent. They promise the blessings of the Garden of Eden, but they plan to transform the world into a gigantic post office. Every man but one a subordinate clerk in a bureau, what an alluring utopia! What a noble cause to fight for! (ibid., page 125.)

In 1947 Ludwig von Mises joined the staff of The Foundation for Economic Education which Leonard E. Read had just organized. Their association and friendship, which began for an end, continued to the end. Their joint efforts were to make the Foundation in Irvington-on-Hudson an intellectual center of the reform movement, which at the time of Mises's death was to reach every phase of American social and economic thought.

As one of its first publications, the Foundation issued Mises's *Planned Chaos* (1947). It is a brief analysis of the problems of social cooperation in a postwar setting. German Nazism, Italian Fascism, and Japanese imperialism had been crushed by the Western democracies, especially the United States, whose privately owned industries had provided the war material for the Allied victory. The only tyranny that survived the holocaust of the war was its red prototype in Russia. It constitutes a staggering menace to the West, not only as a military power, but more importantly as the world center of the ideology of despotic socialism that is so popular with intellectuals and thought leaders. In the words of Mises,

> History will call our age the age of the dictators and tyrants. We have witnessed in the last years the fall of two of these inflated supermen. But the spirit which raised these knaves to autocratic power survives. It permeates textbooks and periodicals; it speaks through the mouths of teachers and politicians; it manifests itself in party programs and in plays and novels. As long as this spirit prevails there cannot be any hope of durable peace, of democracy, the preservation of freedom or of a steady improvement in the nation's economic well-being. (ibid., page 16.)

Two years later Ludwig von Mises's genius of energy and industry brought forth *Human Action* which combined all three of his monumental achievements: the general theory of human action, or "praxeology" as he called it; the construction of an entire body of economic analysis including money on the praxeological foundation; and the integration of his explanations of the business cycle with his economic analysis. The great adversities under which he labored all his life actually forced him to publish his magnum opus twice. In 1940 it had appeared in Switzerland under the title *Nationalökonomie*, and instantly had fallen into oblivion in the chaos of World War II. In 1949 he published it again with expansions and modifications for English-speaking readers as *Human Action*. It was a monumental achievement, the first general treatise on economics since World War I, a magnificent structure built solidly on deductive reasoning and theoretical analysis of human action. It is unquestionably one of the most powerful products of the human mind in our time.

Henry Hazlitt wrote in *Newsweek* magazine of September 19, 1949:

"I know of no other work, in fact, which conveys to the reader so clear an insight into the intimate interconnectedness of all economic phenomena. It makes us recognize why it is impossible to study or understand 'collective bargaining' or 'labor problems' in isolation; or to understand wages apart from prices or from interest rates or from profits and losses, or to understand any of these apart from all the rest, or the price of any one thing apart from the prices of other things. . . . *Human Action* is, in short, at once the most uncompromising and the most rigorously reasoned statement of the case for capitalism that has yet appeared. . . ."

Like all great books, *Human Action* not only is the outpouring of a great mind, but also a harmonious blending of the thoughts and efforts of many predecessors. His great business cycle theory was built on available, but as yet unconnected components: on Ricardo's theory of the flow of gold in response to bank credit expansion or contraction, on Böhm-Bawerk's theory of capital and interest, and finally, on Wicksell's distinction between the natural rate of interest and the market rate as affected by bank credit expansion. His methodological structure, or praxeology, was built on two solid foundations: the deductive reasoning of the great classical economists, especially Senior and Cairnes, and his Austrian predecessors, Menger and Böhm-Bawerk, and on the epistemological studies of Windelband, Rickert and Max Weber of the "Southwest German School" of philosophy which had clearly delineated the scopes and limits of both the natural as well as the "historical" sciences.

Human Action must be compared with another book by a British economist, published one hundred and seventy-three years earlier (1776). It was the foundationwork of modern economic thought, a potent mixture of economics, philosophy, history, political theory, and practical program. It expressed, inspired, and animated the movement toward capitalism and democracy for several generations: *The Wealth of Nations* by Adam Smith. Ludwig von Mises's *Human Action* in scope, conception, and execution is intellectual leadership of a rebirth of that movement. It begins and stands for a new epoch in human thought, therefore in action and policy. And yet, the minds of men will be slow in comprehending its message as they cannot resist the fashions and follies of the age. But as every new generation rejects old fashions and fervently seeks the new, so will the coming generations want to turn from government omnipotence, conflict, and strife. To them *Human Action* will point the way.

After *The Wealth of Nations* had been published, Adam Smith spent the rest of his life as commissioner of customs at Edinburgh, living quietly with his mother and a maiden cousin, and enjoying the company of a small circle of friends. After *Human Action* had appeared, Ludwig von Mises continued to pour his heart and soul into his work. He was happiest in his work, without hesitation, relaxation, or boasting. In 1951, he presented a paper at the Mont Pelerin Society which was published under the title, *Profit and Loss*. In 1952, a collection of essays and addresses appeared as *Planning for Freedom*. It was followed by *The Anti-Capitalistic Mentality* in 1956, *Theory and History* in 1957, *The Ultimate Foundation of Economic Science: An Essay on Method* in 1962, and *The Historical Setting of the Austrian School of Economics* in 1969. The enthusiastic response which his books met, especially from his younger students and followers all over the United States, caused them to translate and publish nearly all his earlier German writings or keep them in print.

Profit and Loss and *Planning for Freedom* were aimed at the general public and written as an introduction to his ideas. They discuss such topics as the systems of social organization, interventionism, inflationism, and various aspects of the private property order. But above all, they entreat his followers who cannot help falling prey to darkest pessimism about the future to keep up their hopes for a change. *Ludwig von Mises, Notes and Recollections* vividly describes the debilitating effects of pessimism, which had broken the strength of Carl Menger and overshadowed the life of Max Weber. He, himself, had resolved never to tire in professing what he knew to be right, even in the knowledge of unavoidable catastrophe. In *Planning for Freedom* he warned against the mentality of passively accepting defeat that has made socialism triumph in many European countries. Trends have changed in the past, he urges his readers, and they will change again. But they will not change if nobody has the courage to attack the underlying dogmas. There is hope, he assures us, that the average voter can understand the relationship between economic freedom and wealth, government restrictions and high prices, deficit spending and inflation, capital investment and labor productivity, etc. They will, some day, understand the follies of bad economic policies; it is not merely wishful thinking to express such hopes.

There is ignorance, the greatest of infirmities, which gives perpetuity to error and prejudice. As professor and writer, Mises devoted his life to imparting knowledge and stimulating his students in its love and pursuit. There is irresponsibility, which expresses itself in emphasis on luck, and an emotional submission to fate. It likes to ascribe personal conditions to fate, environment, or the doings of others. There are frustrated ambitions that seek excuse and vindications for failure and disappointment. There is envy and covetousness which have no other virtue but that of detracting from others. What makes so many people unhappy under capitalism, says Professor von Mises, is precisely the fact that individual enterprise grants to each the opportunity to improve his lot. In such a society each man whose ambitions have not been fully satisfied is looking for a scapegoat on whom he can blame his own shortcomings. His favorite culprit may be his employer, the capitalist-entrepreneur who is enjoying better living conditions; or just the existing social order.

All his life Ludwig von Mises opposed those tenets and creeds that had brought about the eclipse of European civilization. He fought the German Historical School, the forerunners of Hitler's National Socialism; and the Marxians, the harbingers of the most ruthless of all dictatorships. In America he was fighting the ascendency of similar ideologies of all-round regimentation. When the circle of American readers came to appreciate the fundamental importance of his writings, he returned to his philosophical studies. *Theory and History*; *The Ultimate Foundation of Economic Science: An Essay on Method*; and *The Historical Setting of the Austrian School of Economics*, which were published between 1957 and 1969, embody the creative energy of his remaining years. (*Theory and History* was reprinted in October 1976 by Arlington House.)

Theory and History makes further contributions to the theory of knowledge and, in this sense, is a supplement to *Human Action*. With a revolutionary breakthrough of insight, the latter had placed economic problems within the broad frame of a general theory of human action, and thus had ended the traditional isolation of economic discussions. It had made economics a mere segment of a general science of human action, called praxeology. In *Theory and History* Professor von Mises reached out for a general epistemology applicable to all branches of human knowledge. Substantive knowledge depends on epistemological analysis; in turn, epistemology is accessible only through knowledge in the respective field. As the treatment of the substantive issues of each science cannot be separated from an analysis of its particular epistemological problems, so can human knowledge in general not be divorced from general epistemology.

The Ultimate Foundation of Economic Science, published in 1962, was a further commentary on what economics itself says about its own epistemology. Professor von Mises takes issue especially with positivism, which does not acknowledge any other truth than that established by the experimental natural science. Positivism rejects all other methods of rational discourse as metaphysical, which is interpreted as synonymous with nonsensical. The essay explodes this fundamental thesis of positivism and points up its disastrous consequences.

Ludwig von Mises's writings that were translated from the German now are conveying his important messages in the language of the world. They are speaking to the intellectuals of all races and nationalities—to philosophers, historians and economists, to writers and literati—to anyone who will listen. And through the prefaces and epilogues to the new editions that provide a contemporary setting for his basic messages, he is speaking especially to us.

The Free and Prosperous Commonwealth, published in 1962 by D. Van Nostrand & Company, which was translated by Ralph Raico from the German *Liberalismus* (1927), gives a summary of the ideas and principles of nineteenth-century liberalism for the general reader. The very fact that the English edition had to forgo the grand old name of "liberalism" and resort to a descriptive title is very revealing. Dr. von Mises did not yield readily, not even in language and terminology. But it cannot be denied that American "liberalism" now denotes a set of ideas and political postulates that are diametrically opposed to those held by earlier generations. American liberals are resolute foes of free enterprise, and militant advocates of all-round planning by the authorities—that is, socialism.

In his search for truth, which is the foundation of all knowledge, Ludwig von Mises was unyielding to the end. He brought new knowledge to the meaning of truth and its modes of application, and shed new light on the path of human action.

His Enduring Monument

Though a great man may die and disappear, his thoughts and acts survive and leave an indelible stamp upon his fellowmen. Ludwig von

Mises has left the stage of the grand theater, which is life, but his work is living on and extending his being in the prospect of an immortal existence. His labors were merely the beginning of a long chain of consequences, and no man can know what the end will be. His influence is felt as an effective intellectual force of philosophical, economic and political reformation. He revived, generated, guided, or influenced a great number of intellectual currents that comprise, in contemporary parlance, the "conservative" intellectual movement in America.

He never called himself a "conservative." For him, change and transformation that continually alter the external conditions of life were essential features of life. Man must ever adjust anew to the modifications which a minority of alert pioneers initiate. Therefore, "conservatism is contrary to the very nature of human acting." Conservatism is the avowed aim of all utopian movements, which would like to put an end to history and establish a final and permanent calm.

He always saw himself as a "liberal," that is, a "classical liberal," who was not about to abandon this grand old name simply because it was unpopular or others sought to usurp it. But he also conceded that issues of terminology are of secondary importance only, which should not stand in the way of cooperation among all friends of the private property order.

In 1940, when Ludwig von Mises first set foot on American soil, classical liberalism was all but dead in the world of overweening statism and entrenched bureaucracy. But in less than a decade Professor von Mises, together with a participant of his Vienna "private seminar," Friedrich von Hayek, provided a powerful impetus for a renaissance of American individualism. Hayek's *The Road to Serfdom* (1944), which attained great popularity and engendered passionate debates, restated the issue between liberty and authority. It was a loud warning about the direction in which the Western world had been moving, at first slowly, but then with accelerating speed. This slim book, together with Mises's *Bureaucracy* and *Omnipotent Government*, provided intellectual sustenance and leadership to the small remnant of American defenders. When *Human Action* appeared in 1949, it became the solid foundation on which the classical revival could be built.

Surely, there were several others who, independent of the Austrians, were guarding the great American tradition of individualism and the private property order. John T. Flynn, in *As We Go Marching* (1945), was conveying the very message of Hayek's *The Road to Serfdom*; Garet Garrett was fiercely denouncing the New Deal in his *The Revolution Was* (1944); and Albert Jay Nock was sounding the alarm about the political and social decay and the impending doom of civilized society. Frank Chodorov was reviving *The Freeman* under the auspices of the Henry George School, which he was directing, and writers such as Henry Hazlitt, John Davenport, Mortimer Smith, William Henry Chamberlin and John Chamberlain were pleading the case of individual freedom. But all this classical-liberal stirring during the 1940s and 1950s was mainly a journalistic affair that was visible in journals like *Analysis* and *The Freeman*, and later *Human Events*. It was not associated with colleges and universities and did not reach the professional quarterlies. In the world of academe the philosophical and political fashions of the 1930s continued to be in vogue. Even some graduates of Professor von Mises's "private seminar," who before the war had reached the United States shores and attained academic positions, chose to be fashionable rather than "doctrinaire." Not only did they frequently disassociate themselves from their teacher's laissez-faire, seeking "moderation" in economic and political issues and voicing distrust in his "rationalistic" epistemology and praxeology, some even joined the popular camp of logical positivism and the new economics of Lord Keynes.

Some men give up their designs in order to be popular. To Ludwig von Mises virtue was in the pursuit of truth, not in the prize. He labored, endured and waited, always holding on to his design. He was inner-directed, which made him shun security, conformity, and acceptance by the crowd. And yet, he soon could witness a slow reorientation of public sentiment and the beginning of an intellectual movement in which he played an important part.

In 1947 he and others joined Friedrich von Hayek in forming the Mont Pelerin Society, an international society of classical-liberal scholars dedicated to the preservation and improvement of the free society. During its early years it served as the rallying point for the international forces of classical liberalism, where ideas were exchanged and friendships formed. By exposing its members to the wider currents of thought and problems, the Society made them more cosmopolitan and more conscious of their common interests. At their conferences the members, several of whom had studied with Professor von Mises, presented papers and reports, and engaged in friendly debates and discussions.

To Professor von Mises the Mont Pelerin Society, which at first offered hope and promise, proved to be disappointing in the end. While the Society grew considerably in membership, counting more than two hundred by 1960, its ideological composition and flavor began to change. Through indiscriminate admission of logical positivists and economic interventionists, the papers presented and the discussions that followed, in the eyes of Professor von Mises, deteriorated in character and quality. Therefore, during the 1960s he withdrew from active participation and stayed away from some of its meetings.

He held the Intercollegiate Society of Individualists (ISI) in high esteem and liked to associate with its members. ISI was founded by Frank Chodorov in 1953 as an antidote to the Intercollegiate Society of Socialists of an earlier generation, and was seeking to reach the college youth through publications and lectures. It worked through its chapters and its affiliations on more than one hundred college and university campuses, in order to present an ideological alternative to the prevailing collectivist trend in higher education. Invited by ISI, Professor von Mises lectured to many student assemblies from coast to coast, planting rich seeds in the knowledge that the destiny of mankind depends on the opinions of its youth.

Mises was keenly aware that the "conservative" intellectual movement in America comprises certain ideological currents that do not flow from classical-liberal heritage. There were the "traditionalists" who were proposing to read history anew and find the characteristics of Western civilization that are essential and immutable. Man's propensity to evil and the nightmare of totalitarianism, genocide, and total war, had shaken the best of men and led them to analyze the crisis of civilization. They were searching for the sources of Western decadence, so that civilization could be rebuilt on a more solid foundation of transcendental value and truth. Tracing the declension back through centuries of ideas, they usually arrived at two ominous turning points: the Renaissance-Reformation period and the French Revolution. With no stone left unturned, nearly everything came in for a share of the blame: liberalism, collectivism, utilitarianism, positivism, individualism, egalitarianism, pragmatism, socialism, capitalism, industrialism, Protestantism, and ideology itself.

To Ludwig von Mises all such collections of historical data make a man wise and judicious, but unfortunately fail to teach him anything that is valid for all human action. Historical experience is open to various interpretations, and usually is assessed in different ways. Differences in basic judgments of value and significance may lead to as many interpretations and conclusions as there are traditionalists making them. History deals with complex phenomena, which cannot be used to predict future action or be utilized for handling concrete tasks. How can historical knowledge inform us on what the rate of interest should be, today or tomorrow, or whether government or the owners should regulate an airline's rates and schedules? It is a grievous error of epistemology to believe that all human knowledge is derived from experience or its selective magnifier, tradition. There is praxeology, a theoretic and systematic source of knowledge, irrespective of all environmental, concrete acts. Its propositions are not derived from experience, and are not subject to verification by historical interpretation. Unfortunately, most historians and philosophers searching for truth and eternal values are completely ignorant of praxeology and its most developed part, which is economics.

And yet, the conservative intellectual movement gradually grew in economic understanding during the 1950s and 1960s. The economics of Ludwig von Mises was spreading in widening circles through the conservative coalition, which was achieving a political identity. Spearheaded by such able writers as William F. Buckley, Frank S. Meyer, Wilhelm Röpke, M. Stanton Evans, William Henry Chamberlin, and others, the dissemination often proceeded by a circuitous route, from the teacher through his students and disciples, to the "fusionists" and finally the "traditionalists." Professor Röpke best expressed the theme of the growing conservative consensus: "The market economy is the economic order proper to a definite social structure and to a definite spiritual and moral setting." Professor von Mises could endorse such a statement of economic and moral principle.

The question of the relation of religious faith to economics arose again when Ayn Rand shook the conservative world with her forceful novels. In her *Atlas Shrugged* (1957), which sold well over a million copies within a few years, she introduced the world to a combination of Misesian economics and her own system of philosophy, objectivism.

Surely, Mises could agree with Rand's vivid descriptions of the wickedness of the welfare state and the virtues of the unhampered market order. And he could appreciate Rand's great popularity with American youth to whom she, more than anyone else, introduced Misesian economics. Mises and Rand would agree on reprobating the ideas of many

Christian churches that are rejecting the private property order and calling for political coercion and economic redistribution. They were united in their opposition to egalitarian measures that impede the formation of capital, thereby impairing the working and living conditions of wage earners. Relentlessly Mises and Rand emphasized their opposition to the ideas of Hegelian philosophy, which endow the state with "divine will," and rejected all ideologies that would nurture the cult of the "State" and the cult of "Society."

For a society to prosper, it must be built on foundations of knowledge and moral character. "What is needed to stop the trend toward socialism and despotism," Mises concluded in his essay, *Planned Chaos*, "is common sense and moral courage." He himself was pursuing this common sense in economics as, in his judgment, its lack is visited as sharply as immorality. His grand structure was deductive knowledge which as such abstains from any judgment of value. It did not permit him to tell people what ends they should pursue. To him, that was beyond the scope of any science. But it did show how a man must act if he wants to attain definite ends, and how he must organize society in order to live in freedom and prosperity in a peaceful world; that is, he must establish an unhampered market society through laissez faire.

Throughout his long life Ludwig von Mises anxiously observed an almost continuous advance of socialism, which he opposed with all his strength and ability. He resisted every step of ill-conceived, counter-productive government intervention that invariably makes matters worse, inviting further government intervention until all economic production is centrally run or controlled. Ludwig von Mises spoke and wrote of the limitations of government and the ideals of classical liberalism in order to pave the way for a resurrection of individual freedom and the unhampered market order.

And yet, the world-wide trend toward socialism and despotism continued with growing force. In despair and revolt some of his youthful disciples reacted by venturing beyond the ideals of "limited government" and seeking refuge in the land of "anarchy." If the limitation of state power is eminently beneficial, as Mises demonstrated so convincingly, its total abolition must be even more salutary. If government intervention in economic life is detrimental and counter-productive, they bravely concluded, government as such is baneful and, therefore, should be abolished summarily.

Ludwig von Mises's answer was immediate and unequivocal:

Government as such is not only not an evil, but the most necessary and beneficial institution, as without it no lasting cooperation and no civilization could be developed and preserved. (*The Ultimate Foundation of Economic Science*, page 98.)

And a year later, he added three concise pages on freedom and pacifism to the second revised edition of *Human Action*. In his own words:

In a world full of unswerving aggressors and enslavers, integral unconditional pacifism is tantamount to unconditional surrender to the most ruthless oppressors. He who wants to remain free, must fight unto death those who are intent upon depriving him of his freedom. As isolated attempts on the part of each individual to resist are doomed to failure, the only workable way is to organize resistance by the government. The essential task of government is defense of the social system not only against domestic gangsters but also against external foes. He who in our age opposes armaments and conscription is, perhaps unbeknown to himself, an abettor of those aiming at the enslavement of all.

The maintenance of a government apparatus of courts, police officers, prisons, and of armed forces requires considerable expenditure. To levy taxes for these purposes is fully compatible with the freedom the individual enjoys in a free market economy. (*Human Action*, second edition, Yale University Press, New Haven, Connecticut, 1963, page 282; third edition, Henry Regnery Company, Chicago, Illinois, 1966, also page 282.)

To preserve individual freedom and the light of civilization—that was Ludwig von Mises's hope and dedication. As we do not have a knowledge of things to come, we cannot perceive the future range and power of the beacon of reason which he sent out into the world. But we do know that the present generation is affected by what he was, said, and did. And through his students and colleagues his sphere of influence is spreading in widening circles through humanity. He played an important role in the reconstruction of the market order in postwar Europe. Wilhelm Röpke, who was greatly influenced by his ideas, gave intellectual guidance and support to West Germany's recovery from the ashes of totalitarian socialism. In France, Mises's fellow Neoclassicist, Jacques Rueff, advised General DeGaulle on economic policies of stabilization and return to the gold standard. In Italy, President Luigi Einaudi, a life-long friend and colleague of Mises, succeeded for many years in stemming the tide of inflationism and socialism. In many other countries, from Japan to Guatemala, from Argentina to Spain, his students and disciples are imparting Misesian knowledge and stimulating their fellowmen in its love and pursuit.

Ludwig von Mises, Notes and Recollections is a splendid record of his trials and tribulations in Europe. It is a memorial of Ludwig von Mises, the man, who faced life with fortitude, patience, and honor.

Hans F. Sennholz
Grove City, Pennsylvania
September 12, 1976

꧁ The Historical Setting of
the Austrian School of
Economics

I

Carl Menger and the Austrian School of Economics

1   The Beginnings

What is known as the Austrian School of Economics started in 1871 when Carl Menger published a slender volume under the title *Grundsätze der Volkswirtschaftslehre.*[1]

It is customary to trace the influence that the milieu exerted upon the achievements of genius. People like to ascribe the exploits of a man of genius, at least to some extent, to the operation of his environment and to the climate of opinion of his age and his country. Whatever this method may accomplish in some cases, there is no doubt that it is inapplicable with regard to those Austrians whose thoughts, ideas, and doctrines matter for mankind. Bernard Bolzano, Gregor Mendel, and Sigmund Freud were not stimulated by their relatives, teachers, colleagues, or friends. Their exertions did not meet with sympathy on the part of their contemporary countrymen and the government of their country. Bolzano and Mendel carried on their main work in surroundings which, as far as their special fields are concerned, could be called an intellectual desert, and they died long before people began to divine the worth of their contributions. Freud was laughed at when he first made public his doctrines in the Vienna Medical Association.

One may say that the theory of subjectivism and marginalism that Carl Menger developed was in the air. It had been foreshadowed by several forerunners. Besides, about the same time Menger wrote and published his book, William Stanley Jevons and Léon Walras also wrote and published books which expounded the concept of marginal

1. *Principles of Economics* (The Free Press, 1950).

utility. However this may be, it is certain that none of his teachers, friends, or colleagues took any interest in the problems that excited Menger. When, some time before the outbreak of the first World War, I told him about the informal, but regular meetings in which we younger Vienna economists used to discuss problems of economic theory, he pensively observed: "When I was your age, nobody in Vienna cared about these things." Until the end of the 1870s there was no "Austrian School." There was only Carl Menger.

Eugen von Böhm-Bawerk and Friedrich von Wieser never studied with Menger. They had finished their studies at the University of Vienna before Menger began to lecture as a *Privatdozent*. What they learned from Menger, they got from studying the *Grundsätze*. When they returned to Austria after some time spent at German universities, especially in the seminar of Karl Knies in Heidelberg, and published their first books, they were appointed to teach economics at the Universities of Innsbruck and Prague respectively. Very soon some younger men who had gone through Menger's seminar, and had been exposed to his personal influence, enlarged the number of authors who contributed to economic inquiry. People abroad began to refer to these authors as "the Austrians." But the designation "Austrian School of Economics" was used only later, when their antagonism to the German Historical School came into the open after the publication, in 1883, of Menger's second book, *Untersuchungen über die Methode der Sozialwissenschaften und der Politischen Oekonomie insbesondere.*[2]

2 The Austrian School of Economics and the Austrian Universities

The Austrian Cabinet in whose journalistic department Menger served in the early 1870s — before his appointment in 1873 as assistant professor at the University of Vienna — was composed of members of the Liberal Party that stood for civil liberties, representative government, equality of all citizens under the law, sound money, and free trade. At the end of the 1870s the Liberal Party was evicted by an alliance of the Church,

2. English translation (University of Illinois Press, 1963); republished 1985 as *Investigations into the Method of the Social Sciences with Special Reference to Economics* (New York University Press, 1985).

the princes and counts of the Czech and Polish aristocracy, and the nationalist parties of the various Slavonic nationalities. This coalition was opposed to all the ideals which the Liberals had supported. However, until the disintegration of the Habsburg Empire in 1918, the Constitution which the Liberals had induced the Emperor to accept in 1867 and the fundamental laws that complemented it remained by and large valid.

In the climate of freedom that these statutes warranted, Vienna became a center of the harbingers of new ways of thinking. From the middle of the sixteenth to the end of the eighteenth century Austria was foreign to the intellectual effort of Europe. Nobody in Vienna— and still less in other parts of the Austrian Dominions—cared for the philosophy, literature, and science of Western Europe. When Leibniz and later David Hume visited Vienna, no indigenes were to be found there who would have been interested in their work.* With the exception of Bolzano, no Austrian before the second part of the nineteenth century contributed anything of importance to the philosophical or the historical sciences.

But when the Liberals had removed the fetters that had prevented any intellectual effort, when they had abolished censorship and had denounced the concordat, eminent minds began to converge toward Vienna. Some came from Germany—like the philosopher Franz Brentano and the lawyers and philosophers Lorenz von Stein and Rudolf von Jhering—but most of them came from the Austrian provinces; a few were born Viennese. There was no conformity among these leaders, nor among their followers. Brentano, the ex-Dominican, inaugurated a line of thought that finally led to Husserl's phenomenology. Mach was the exponent of a philosophy that resulted in the logical positivism of Schlick, Carnap, and their "Vienna Circle." Breuer, Freud, and Adler interpreted neurotic phenomena in a way radically different from the methods of Krafft-Ebing and Wagner-Jauregg.

The Austrian "Ministry of Worship and Instruction" looked askance upon all these endeavors. Since the early 1880s the Cabinet Minister and the personnel of this department had been chosen from the most reliable conservatives and foes of all modern ideas and political institutions. They had nothing but contempt for what in their eyes were

---

* The only contemporary Viennese who appreciated the philosophic work of Leibniz was Prince Eugene of Savoy, scion of a French family, born and educated in France.

"outlandish fads." They would have liked to bar the universities from access to all this innovation.

But the power of the administration was seriously restricted by three "privileges" which the universities had acquired under the impact of the Liberal ideas. The professors were civil servants and, like all other civil servants, bound to obey the orders issued by their superiors, i.e., the Cabinet Minister and his aides. However, these superiors did not have the right to interfere with the content of the doctrines taught in the classes and seminars; in this regard the professors enjoyed the much talked about "academic freedom." Furthermore, the Minister was obliged—although this obligation had never been unambiguously stated—to comply in appointing professors (or, to speak more precisely, in suggesting to the Emperor the appointment of a professor) with the suggestions made by the faculty concerned. Finally there was the institution of the *Privatdozent*. A doctor who had published a scholarly book could ask the faculty to admit him as a free and private teacher of his discipline; if the faculty decided in favor of the petitioner, the consent of the Minister was still required; in practice this consent was, before the days of the Schuschnigg regime, always given.[3] The duly admitted *Privatdozent* was not, in this capacity, a civil servant. Even if the title of professor was accorded to him, he did not receive any compensation from the government. A few *Privatdozents* could live from their own funds. Most of them worked for their living. Their right to collect the fees paid by the students who attended their courses was in most cases practically valueless.

The effect of this arrangement of academic affairs was that the councils of the professors enjoyed almost unlimited autonomy in the management of their schools. Economics was taught at the Schools of Law and Social Sciences (*Rechts und staatswissenschaftliche Fakultäten*) of the universities. At most of these universities there were two chairs of economics. If one of these chairs became vacant, a body of lawyers had—with the cooperation, at most, of one economist—to choose the future incumbent. Thus the decision rested with non-economists. It may be fairly assumed that these professors of law were guided by the best intentions. But they were not economists. They had to choose between two opposed schools of thought, the "Austrian School" on the one hand, and the allegedly "modern" historical school as taught at

3. Kurt von Schuschnigg, Chancellor of Austria from 1934 to 1938.

the universities of the German Reich on the other hand. Even if no political and nationalistic prepossessions had disturbed their judgment, they could not help becoming somewhat suspicious of a line of thought which the professors of the universities of the German Reich dubbed specifically Austrian. Never before had any new mode of thinking originated in Austria. The Austrian universities had been sterile until — after the revolution of 1848 — they had been reorganized according to the model of the German universities. For people who were not familiar with economics, the predicate "Austrian" as applied to a doctrine carried strong overtones of the dark days of the Counter-Reformation and of Metternich. To an Austrian intellectual, nothing could appear more disastrous than a relapse of his country into the spiritual inanity of the good old days.

Carl Menger, Wieser, and Böhm-Bawerk had obtained their chairs in Vienna, Prague, and Innsbruck before the *Methodenstreit* [struggle over methods] had begun to appear in the opinion of the Austrian laymen as a conflict between "modern" science and Austrian "backwardness." Their colleagues had no personal grudge against them. But whenever possible they tried to bring followers of the historical school from Germany to the Austrian universities. Those whom the world called the "Austrian Economists" were, in the Austrian universities, somewhat reluctantly tolerated outsiders.

3   The Austrian School in the Intellectual Life of Austria

The more distinguished among the French and German universities were, in the great age of liberalism, not merely institutions of learning that provided the rising generations of professional people with the instruction required for the satisfactory practice of their professions. They were centers of culture. Some of their teachers were known and admired all over the world. Their courses were attended not only by the regular students who planned to take academic degrees but by many mature men and women who were active in the professions, in business, or in politics and expected from the lectures nothing but intellectual gratification. For instance, such outsiders, who were not students in a technical sense, thronged the courses of Renan, Fustel de Coulanges, and Bergson in Paris, and those of Hegel, Helmholtz, Mommsen, and Treitschke in Berlin. The educated public was seriously interested in the work of the academic circles. The elite read the books and the magazines published by the professors, joined their scholastic societies and eagerly followed the discussions of the meetings.

Some of these amateurs who devoted only leisure hours to their studies rose high above the level of dilettantism. The history of modern science records the names of many such glorious "outsiders." It is, for instance, a characteristic fact that the only remarkable, although not epoch-making, contribution to economics that originated in the Germany of the second Reich came from a busy corporation counsel, Heinrich Oswalt from Frankfurt, a city that at the time his book was written had no university.*

In Vienna, also, close association of the university teachers with the cultured public of the city prevailed in the last decades of the nineteenth century and in the beginning of our [twentieth] century. It began to vanish when the old masters died or retired and men of smaller stature got their chairs. This was the period in which the rank of the Vienna University, as well as the cultural eminence of the city, was upheld and enlarged by a few of the *Privatdozents*. The outstanding case is that of psychoanalysis. It never got any encouragement from any official institution; it grew and thrived outside the university and its only connection with the bureaucratic hierarchy of learning was the fact that Freud was a *Privatdozent* with the meaningless title of professor.

There was in Vienna, as a heritage of the years in which the founders of the Austrian school had finally earned recognition, a lively interest in problems of economics. This interest enabled the present writer to organize a *Privatseminar* in the 1920s, to start the Economic Association, and to set up the Austrian Institute for Trade Cycle Research, that later changed its name to the Austrian Institute for Economic Research.

The *Privatseminar* had no connection whatever with the University or any other institution. Twice a month a group of scholars, among them several *Privatdozents*, met in the present writer's office in the Austrian Chamber of Commerce. Most of the participants belonged to the age group that had begun academic studies after the end of the first World War. Some were older. They were united by a burning interest in the whole field of the sciences of human action. In the

---

* Cf. H. Oswalt, *Vorträge über wirtschaftliche Grundbegriffe*, 3rd ed. (Jena, 1920).

debates problems of philosophy, of epistemology, of economic theory, and of the various branches of historical research were treated. The *Privatseminar* was discontinued when, in 1934, the present writer was appointed to the chair of international economic relations at the Graduate Institute of International Studies in Geneva, Switzerland.

With the exception of Richard von Strigl, whose early death put an untimely end to a brilliant scientific career, and Ludwig Bettelheim-Gabillon, about whom we will have more to say, all the members of the *Privatseminar* found a proper field for the continuation of their work as scholars, authors, and teachers outside of Austria.

In the realm of the spirit, Vienna played an eminent role in the years between the establishment of the Parliament in the early 1860s and the invasion of the Nazis in 1938. The flowering came suddenly after centuries of sterility and apathy. The decay had already begun many years before the Nazis intruded.

In all nations and in all periods of history, intellectual exploits were the work of a few men and were appreciated only by a small elite. The many looked upon these feats with hatred and disdain; at best with indifference. In Austria and in Vienna the elite was especially small; and the hatred of the masses and their leaders especially vitriolic.

4   Böhm-Bawerk and Wieser as Members of the Austrian Cabinet

The unpopularity of economics is the result of its analysis of the effects of privileges. It is impossible to invalidate the economists' demonstration that all privileges hurt the interests of the rest of the nation or at least of a great part of it, that those victimized will tolerate the existence of such privileges only if privileges are granted to them too, and that then, when everybody is privileged, nobody wins but everybody loses on account of the resulting general drop in the productivity of labor.* However, the warnings of the economists are disregarded by the covetousness of people who are fully aware of their inability to succeed in a competitive market without the aid of special privileges. They are confident that they will get more valuable privileges than other groups or that they will be in a position to prevent, at least for some time, any

---

* Cf. Mises, *Human Action* (1949), pp. 712–857 [pp. 716–861 in later editions].

granting of compensatory privileges to other groups. In their eyes the economist is simply a mischief-maker who wants to upset their plans.

When Menger, Böhm-Bawerk, and Wieser began their scientific careers, they were not concerned with the problems of economic policies and with the rejection of interventionism by Classical economics. They considered it as their vocation to put economic theory on a sound basis and they were ready to dedicate themselves entirely to this cause. Menger heartily disapproved of the interventionist policies that the Austrian Government—like almost all governments of the epoch—had adopted. But he did not believe that he could contribute to a return to good policies in any other way than by expounding good economics in his books and articles as well as in his university teaching.

Böhm-Bawerk joined the staff of the Austrian Ministry of Finance in 1890. Twice he served for a short time as Minister of Finance in a caretaker cabinet. From 1900 to 1904 he was Minister of Finance in the cabinet headed by Ernest von Körber. Böhm's principles in the conduct of this office were: strict maintenance of the legally fixed gold parity of the currency, and a budget balanced without any aid from the central bank. An eminent scholar, Ludwig Bettelheim-Gabillon, planned to publish a comprehensive work analyzing Böhm-Bawerk's activity in the Ministry of Finance. Unfortunately the Nazis killed the author and destroyed his manuscript.*

Wieser was for some time during the first World War Minister of Commerce in the Austrian Cabinet. However, his activity was rather impeded by the far-reaching powers—already given before Wieser took office—to a functionary of the ministry, Richard Riedl. Virtually only matters of secondary importance were left to the jurisdiction of Wieser himself.

---

* Only two chapters, which the author had published before the Anschluss, are preserved: "Böhm-Bawerk und die Brüsseler Zuckerkonvention" and "Böhm-Bawerk und die Konvertierung von Obligationen der einheitlichen Staatsschuld" in *Zeitschrift für Nationalökonomie*, Vol. VII and VIII (1936 and 1937).

II

The Conflict with the
German Historical School

---

1   The German Rejection of Classical Economics

The hostility that the teachings of Classical economic theory encountered on the European continent was primarily caused by political
prepossessions. Political economy as developed by several generations
of English thinkers, brilliantly expounded by Hume and Adam Smith
and perfected by Ricardo, was the most exquisite outcome of the philosophy of the Enlightenment. It was the gist of the liberal doctrine
that aimed at the establishment of representative government and
equality of all individuals under the law. It was not surprising that it
was rejected by all those whose privileges it attacked. This propensity
to spurn economics was considerably strengthened in Germany by the
rising spirit of nationalism. The narrow-minded repudiation of Western
civilization—philosophy, science, political doctrine and institutions,
art and literature—which finally resulted in Nazism, originated in a
passionate detraction of British political economy.

However, one must not forget that there were also other grounds for
this revolt against political economy. This new branch of knowledge
raised epistemological and philosophical problems for which the scholars did not find a satisfactory solution. It could not be integrated into
the traditional system of epistemology and methodology. The empiricist tendency that dominates Western philosophy suggested considering economics as an experimental science like physics and biology.
The very idea that a discipline dealing with "practical" problems like
prices and wages could have an epistemological character different
from that of other disciplines dealing with practical matters, was beyond the comprehension of the age. But on the other hand, only the

most bigoted positivists failed to realize that experiments could not be performed in the field about which economics tries to provide knowledge.

We do not have to deal here with the state of affairs as it developed in the age of the neopositivism or hyperpositivism of the twentieth century. Today, all over the world, but first of all in the United States, hosts of statisticians are busy in institutes devoted to what people believe is "economic research." They collect figures provided by governments and various business units, rearrange, readjust, and reprint them, compute averages and draw charts. They surmise that they are thereby "measuring" mankind's "behavior" and that there is no difference worth mentioning between their methods of investigation and those applied in the laboratories of physical, chemical, and biological research. They look with pity and contempt upon those economists who, as they say, like the botanists of "antiquity," rely upon "much speculative thinking" instead of upon "experiments."* And they are fully convinced that out of their restless exertion there will one day emerge final and complete knowledge that will enable the planning authority of the future to make all people perfectly happy.

But with the economists of the first part of the nineteenth century, the misconstruction of the fundamentals of the sciences of human action did not yet go so far. Their attempts to deal with the epistemological problems of economics resulted, of course, in complete failure. Yet, in retrospect, we may say that this frustration was a necessary step on the way that led toward a more satisfactory solution of the problem. It was John Stuart Mill's abortive treatment of the methods of the moral sciences that unwittingly exposed the futility of all arguments advanced in favor of the empiricist interpretation of the nature of economics.

When Germans began to study the works of British Classical economics, they accepted without any qualms the assumption that economic theory is derived from experience. But this simple explanation could not satisfy those who disagreed with the conclusions which, from the Classical doctrine, had to be inferred for political action. They very soon raised questions: Is not the experience from which the British

* Cf. Arthur F. Burns, *The Frontiers of Economic Knowledge* (Princeton University Press, 1954), p. 189.

authors derived their theorems different from the experience which would have faced a German author? Is not British economics defective on account of the fact that the material of experience from which it is distilled was only Great Britain and only Great Britain of the Hanoverian Georges? Is there, after all, such a thing as an economic science valid for all countries, nations, and ages?

It is obvious how these three questions were answered by those who considered economics as an experimental discipline. But such an answer was tantamount to the apodictic negation of economics as such. The Historical School would have been consistent if it had rejected the very idea that such a thing as a science of economics is possible, and if it had scrupulously abstained from making any statements other than reports about what had happened at a definite moment of the past in a definite part of the earth. An anticipation of the effects to be expected from a definite event can be made only on the basis of a theory that claims general validity and not merely validity for what happened in the past in a definite country. The Historical School emphatically denied that there are economic theorems of such a universal validity. But this did not prevent them from recommending or rejecting—in the name of science—various opinions or measures necessarily designed to affect future conditions.

There was, e.g., the Classical doctrine concerning the effects of free trade and protection. The critics did not embark upon the (hopeless) task of discovering some false syllogisms in the chain of Ricardo's reasoning. They merely asserted that "absolute" solutions are not conceivable in such matters. There are historical situations, they said, in which the effects brought about by free trade or protection differ from those described by the "abstract" theory of "armchair" authors. To support their view they referred to various historical precedents. In doing this, they blithely neglected to consider that historical facts, being always the joint result of the operation of a multitude of factors, cannot prove or disprove any theorem.

Thus economics in the second German Reich, as represented by the government-appointed university professors, degenerated into an unsystematic, poorly assorted collection of various scraps of knowledge borrowed from history, geography, technology, jurisprudence, and party politics, larded with depreciatory remarks about the errors in the "abstractions" of the Classical school. Most of the professors more or less eagerly made propaganda in their writings and in their courses for the policies of the Imperial Government: authoritarian conservatism, *Sozialpolitik,* protectionism, huge armaments, and aggressive nationalism. It would be unfair to consider this intrusion of politics into the treatment of economics as a specifically German phenomenon. It was ultimately caused by the viciousness of the epistemological interpretation of economic theory, a failing that was not limited to Germany.

A second factor that made nineteenth-century Germany in general and especially the German universities look askance upon British political economy was its preoccupation with wealth and its relation to the utilitarian philosophy.

The then-prevalent definitions of political economy described it as the science dealing with the production and distribution of wealth. Such a discipline could be nothing but despicable in the eyes of German professors. The professors thought of themselves as people self-denyingly engaged in the pursuit of pure knowledge and not, like the hosts of banausic money-makers, caring for earthly possessions. The mere mention of such base things as wealth and money was taboo among people boasting of their high culture (*Bildung*). The professors of economics could preserve their standing in the circles of their colleagues only by pointing out that the topic of their studies was not the mean concerns of profit-seeking business but historical research, e.g., about the lofty exploits of the Electors of Brandenburg and Kings of Prussia.

No less serious was the matter of utilitarianism. The utilitarian philosophy was not tolerated at German universities. Of the two outstanding German utilitarians, Ludwig Feuerbach never got any teaching job, while Rudolf von Jhering was a teacher of Roman Law. All the misunderstandings that for more than two thousand years have been advanced against Hedonism and Eudaemonism were rehashed by the professors of *Staatswissenschaften* [the political sciences] in their criticism of the British economists.* If nothing else had roused the suspicions of the German scholars, they would have condemned economics for the sole reason that Bentham and the Mills had contributed to it.

---

* Later similar arguments were employed to discredit pragmatism. William James's dictum according to which the pragmatic method aims at bringing out of each word "its practical cash-value" (*Pragmatism,* 1907, p. 53) was quoted to characterize the meanness of the "dollar-philosophy."

2   The Sterility of Germany in the Field of Economics

The German universities were owned and operated by the various kingdoms and grand duchies that formed the Reich.* The professors were civil servants and, as such, had to obey strictly the orders and regulations issued by their superiors, the bureaucrats of the ministries of public instruction. This total and unconditional subordination of the universities and their teachings to the supremacy of the governments was challenged—in vain—by German liberal public opinion, when in 1837 the King of Hanover fired seven professors of the University of Göttingen who protested against the King's breach of the constitution. The governments did not heed the public's reaction. They went on discharging professors with whose political or religious doctrines they did not agree. But after some time they resorted to more subtle and more efficacious methods to make the professors loyal supporters of the official policy. They scrupulously sifted the candidates before appointing them. Only reliable men got the chairs. Thus the question of academic freedom receded into the background. The professors of their own accord taught only what the government permitted them to teach.

The war of 1866 had ended the Prussian constitutional conflict. The King's party—the conservative party of the Junkers, led by Bismarck—triumphed over the Prussian progressive party that stood for parliamentary government, and likewise over the democratic groups of Southern Germany. In the new political setting, first of the *Norddeutscher Bund* [North German Union] and, after 1871, of the *Deutsches Reich* [German Empire], there was no room left for the "alien" doctrines of Manchesterism and laissez faire. The victors of Königgrätz and Sedan thought they had nothing to learn from the "nation of shopkeepers"—the British—or from the defeated French.

At the outbreak of the war of 1870, one of the most eminent German scientists, Emil du Bois-Reymond, boasted that the University of Berlin was "the intellectual bodyguard of the House of Hohenzollern." This did not mean very much for the natural sciences. But it had a very clear and precise meaning for the sciences of human action. The in-

---

* The Reich itself owned and operated only the University of Strassburg. The three German city-republics did not at that period have any university.

cumbents of the chairs of history and of *Staatswissenschaften* (i.e., political science, including all things referring to economics and finance) knew what their sovereign expected of them. And they delivered the goods.

From 1882 to 1907 Friedrich Althoff was in the Prussian ministry of instruction in charge of university affairs. He ruled the Prussian universities as a dictator. As Prussia had the greatest number of lucrative professorships, and therefore offered the most favorable field for ambitious scholars, the professors in the other German states, nay, even those of Austria and Switzerland, aspired to secure positions in Prussia. Thus Althoff could as a rule make them, too, virtually accept his principles and opinions. In all matters pertaining to the social sciences and the historical disciplines, Althoff entirely relied upon the advice of his friend Gustav von Schmoller. Schmoller had an unerring flair for separating the sheep from the goats.

In the second and third quarters of the nineteenth century some German professors wrote valuable contributions to economic theory. It is true that the most remarkable contributions of this period, those of Thünen and of Gossen, were not the work of professors but of men who did not hold teaching jobs. However, the books of Professors Hermann, Mangoldt, and Knies will be remembered in the history of economic thought. But after 1866, the men who came into the academic career had only contempt for "bloodless abstractions." They published historical studies, preferably such as dealt with labor conditions of the recent past. Many of them were firmly convinced that the foremost task of economists was to aid the "people" in the war of liberation they were waging against the "exploiters," and that the God-given leaders of the people were the dynasties, especially the Hohenzollern.

3   The *Methodenstreit*

In the *Untersuchungen*[1] Menger rejected the epistemological ideas that underlay the writings of the Historical School. Schmoller published a rather contemptuous review of this book. Menger reacted, in 1884, with

---

1. First German edition, 1883; English translation, *Investigations into the Method of the Social Sciences with Special Reference to Economics* (University of Illinois, 1963; NYU, 1985).

a pamphlet, *Die Irrtümer des Historismus in der Deutschen National-ökonomie*.[2] The various publications that this controversy engendered are known under the name of the *Methodenstreit*, the clash over methods.

The *Methodenstreit* contributed but little to the clarification of the problems involved. Menger was too much under the sway of John Stuart Mill's empiricism to carry his own point of view to its full logical consequences. Schmoller and his disciples, committed to defend an untenable position, did not even realize what the controversy was about.

The term *Methodenstreit* is, of course, misleading. For the issue was not to discover the most appropriate procedure for the treatment of the problems commonly considered as economic problems. The matter in dispute was essentially whether there could be such a thing as a science, other than history, dealing with aspects of human action.

There was, first of all, radical materialist determinism, a philosophy almost universally accepted in Germany at that time by physicists, chemists, and biologists, although it has never been expressly and clearly formulated. As these people saw it, human ideas, volitions, and actions are produced by physical and chemical events that the natural sciences will one day describe in the same way in which today they describe the emergence of a chemical compound out of the combination of several ingredients. As the only road that could lead to this final scientific accomplishment they advocated experimentation in physiological and biological laboratories.

Schmoller and his disciples passionately rejected this philosophy, not because they were aware of its deficiencies, but because it was incompatible with the religious tenets of the Prussian government. They virtually preferred to it a doctrine that was but little different from Comte's positivism (which, of course, they publicly disparaged on account of its atheism and its French origin). In fact, positivism, sensibly interpreted, must result in materialist determinism. But most of Comte's followers were not outspoken in this regard. Their discussions did not always preclude the conclusion that the laws of social physics (sociology), the establishment of which was in their opinion the highest goal of science, could be discovered by what they called a

---

2. Title translation: The Errors of Historicism in German Economics. No translation known of this pamphlet.

more "scientific" method of dealing with the material assembled by the traditional procedures of the historians. This was the position Schmoller embraced with regard to economics. Again and again he blamed the economists for having prematurely made inferences from quantitatively insufficient material. What, in his opinion, was needed in order to substitute a realistic science of economics for the hasty generalizations of the British "armchair" economists was more statistics, more history, and more collection of "material." Out of the results of such research the economists of the future, he maintained, would one day develop new insights by "induction."

Schmoller was so confused that he failed to see the incompatibility of his own epistemological doctrine and the rejection of positivism's attack upon history. He did not realize the gulf that separated his views from those of the German philosophers who demolished positivism's ideas about the use and the treatment of history—first Dilthey, and later Windelband, Rickert, and Max Weber. In the same article in which he censured Menger's *Grundsätze*, he reviewed also the first important book of Dilthey, his *Einleitung in die Geisteswissenschaften*.[3] But he did not grasp the fact that the tenor of Dilthey's doctrine was the annihilation of the fundamental thesis of his own epistemology, viz., that some laws of social development could be distilled from historical experience.

4   The Political Aspects of the *Methodenstreit*

The British free trade philosophy triumphed in the nineteenth century in the countries of Western and Central Europe. It demolished the shaky ideology of the authoritarian welfare state (*landesfürstlicher Wohlfahrtsstaat*) that had guided the policies of the German principalities in the eighteenth century. Even Prussia turned temporarily toward liberalism. The culmination points of its free trade period were the *Zollverein*'s customs tariff of 1865 and the 1869 Trade Code (*Gewerbeordnung*) for the territory of the *Norddeutscher Bund* (later the *Deutsches Reich*). But very soon the government of Bismarck began to inaugurate its *Sozialpolitik*, the system of interventionist measures such

---

3. Title translation: Introduction to the Moral Sciences. No translation known of this book.

as labor legislation, social security, pro-union attitudes, progressive taxation, protective tariffs, cartels, and dumping.*

If one tries to refute the devastating criticism leveled by economics against the suitability of all these interventionist schemes, one is forced to deny the very existence—not to mention the epistemological claims—of a science of economics, and of praxeology as well. This is what all the champions of authoritarianism, government omnipotence, and "welfare" policies have always done. They blame economics for being "abstract" and advocate a "visualizing" (*anschaulich*) mode of dealing with the problems involved. They emphasize that matters in this field are too complicated to be described in formulas and theorems. They assert that the various nations and races are so different from one another that their actions cannot be comprehended by a uniform theory; there are as many economic theories required as there are nations and races. Others add that even within the same nation or race, economic action is different in various epochs of history. These and similar objections, often incompatible with one another, are advanced in order to discredit economics as such.

In fact, economics disappeared entirely from the universities of the German Empire. There was a lone epigone of Classical economics left at the University of Bonn, Heinrich Dietzel, who, however, never understood what the theory of subjective value meant. At all other universities the teachers were anxious to ridicule economics and the economists. It is not worthwhile to dwell upon the stuff that was handed down as a substitute for economics at Berlin, Munich, and other universities of the Reich. Nobody cares today about all that Gustav von Schmoller, Adolf Wagner, Lujo Brentano, and their numerous adepts wrote in their voluminous books and magazines.

The political significance of the work of the Historical School consisted in the fact that it rendered Germany safe for the ideas, the acceptance of which made popular with the German people all those disastrous policies that resulted in the great catastrophes. The aggressive imperialism that twice ended in war and defeat, the limitless inflation of the early 1920s, the *Zwangswirtschaft* [command economy] and all the horrors of the Nazi regime were achievements of politicians who acted as they had been taught by the champions of the Historical School.

---

* Cf. Mises, *Omnipotent Government* (Yale University Press, 1944), pp. 149 ff.

Schmoller and his friends and disciples advocated what has been called state socialism; i.e., a system of socialism—planning—in which the top management would be in the hands of the Junker aristocracy. It was this brand of socialism at which Bismarck and his successors were aiming. The timid opposition which they encountered on the part of a small group of businessmen was negligible, not so much on account of the fact that these opponents were not numerous, but because their endeavors lacked any ideological backing. There were no longer any liberal thinkers left in Germany. The only resistance that was offered to the party of state socialism came from the Marxian party of the Social Democrats. Like the Schmoller socialists—the socialists of the chair (*Kathedersozialisten*)—the Marxists advocated socialism. The only difference between the two groups was in the choice of the people who should operate the supreme planning board: the Junkers, the professors, and the bureaucracy of Hohenzollern Prussia, or the officers of the Social Democratic party and their affiliated labor unions.

Thus the only serious adversaries whom the Schmoller School had to fight in Germany were the Marxists. In this controversy the latter very soon got the upper hand. For they at least had a body of doctrine, however faulty and contradictory it was, while the teachings of the Historical School were rather the denial of any theory. In search of a modicum of theoretical support, the Schmoller School step by step began to borrow from the spiritual fund of the Marxists. Finally, Schmoller himself largely endorsed the Marxian doctrine of class conflict and of the "ideological" impregnation of thought by the thinker's class membership. One of his friends and fellow professors, Wilhelm Lexis, developed a theory of interest that Engels characterized as a paraphrase of the Marxian theory of exploitation.* It was an effect of the writings of the champions of the *Sozialpolitik* that the epithet "bourgeois" (*bürgerlich*) acquired in the German language an opprobrious connotation.

The crushing defeat in the first World War shattered the prestige of the German princes, aristocrats, and bureaucrats. The adepts of the Historical School and *Sozialpolitik* transferred their loyalty to various splinter groups, out of which the German Nationalist Socialist Workers' Party, the Nazis, eventually emerged.

The straight line that leads from the work of the Historical School

---

* Cf. the more detailed analysis in Mises, *Kritik des Interventionismus*, (Jena, 1929), pp. 92 ff. [English translation, *Critique of Interventionism* (Foundation for Economic Education, 1996).]

to Nazism cannot be shown in sketching the evolution of one of the founders of the School. For the protagonists of the *Methodenstreit* era had finished the course of their lives before the defeat of 1918 and the rise of Hitler. But the life of the outstanding man among the School's second generation illustrates all the phases of German university economics in the period from Bismarck to Hitler.

Werner Sombart was by far the most gifted of Schmoller's students. He was only twenty-five when his master, at the height of the *Methodenstreit*, entrusted him with the job of reviewing and annihilating Wieser's book, *Der natürliche Wert*.[4] The faithful disciple condemned the book as "entirely unsound."[*] Twenty years later Sombart boasted that he had dedicated a good part of his life to fighting for Marx.[†] When the War broke out in 1914, Sombart published a book, *Händler und Helden (Hucksters and Heroes)*.[‡] There, in uncouth and foul language, he rejected everything British or Anglo-Saxon, but above all British philosophy and economics, as a manifestation of a mean jobber mentality. After the war, Sombart revised his book on socialism. Before the war it had been published in nine editions.[§] While the pre-war editions had praised Marxism, the tenth edition fanatically attacked it, especially on account of its "proletarian" character and its lack of patriotism and nationalism. A few years later Sombart tried to revive the *Methodenstreit* by a volume full of invectives against economists whose thought he was unable to understand.[||] Then, when the Nazis seized power, he crowned a literary career of forty-five years by a book on German Socialism. The guiding idea of this work was that the *Führer* gets his orders from God, the supreme *Führer* of the universe, and that *Führertum* is a permanent revelation.[#]

Such was the progress of German academic economics from Schmoller's glorification of the Hohenzollern Electors and Kings to Sombart's canonization of Adolf Hitler.

[*] Cf. *Schmoller's Jahrbuch*, Vol. 13 (1889), pp. 1488–1490.

[†] Cf. Sombart, *Das Lebenswerk von Karl Marx* (Jena, 1909), p. 3.

[‡] Cf. Sombart, *Händler und Helden* (Munich, 1915).

[§] Cf. Sombart, *Der proletarische Sozialismus*, 10th ed. (Jena, 1924), 2 vol.

[||] Cf. Sombart, *Die drei Nationalökonomien* (Munich, 1930).

[#] Cf. Sombart, *Deutscher Sozialismus* (Charlottenburg, 1934), p. 213. (In the American edition: *A New Social Philosophy*, translated and edited by K. F. Geiser [Princeton, 1937], p. 149.) Sombart's achievements were appreciated abroad. Thus, e.g., in 1929 he was elected to honorary membership in the American Economic Association.

[4.] *Natural Value* (Kelley & Millman, 1956).

5   The Liberalism of the Austrian Economists

Plato dreamed of the benevolent tyrant who would entrust the wise philosopher with the power to establish the perfect social system. The Enlightenment did not put its hopes upon the more or less accidental emergence of well-intentioned rulers and provident sages. Its optimism concerning mankind's future was founded upon the double faith in the goodness of man and in his rational mind. In the past a minority of villains—crooked kings, sacrilegious priests, corrupt noblemen— were able to make mischief. But now—according to Enlightenment doctrine—as man has become aware of the power of his reason, a relapse into the darkness and failings of ages gone by is no longer to be feared. Every new generation will add something to the good accomplished by its ancestors. Thus mankind is on the eve of a continuous advance toward more satisfactory conditions. To progress steadily is the nature of man. It is vain to complain about the alleged lost bliss of a fabulous golden age. The ideal state of society is before us, not behind us.

Most of the nineteenth-century liberal, progressive, and democratic politicians who advocated representative government and universal suffrage were guided by a firm confidence in the infallibility of the common man's rational mind. In their eyes majorities could not err. Ideas that originated from the people and were approved by the voters could not but be beneficial to the commonweal.

It is important to realize that the arguments brought forward in favor of representative government by the small group of liberal philosophers were quite different and did not imply any reference to an alleged infallibility of majorities. Hume had pointed out that government is always founded upon opinion. In the long run the opinion of the many always wins out. A government that is not supported by the opinion of the majority must sooner or later lose its power; if it does not abdicate, it is violently overthrown by the many. Peoples have the power eventually to put those men at the helm who are prepared to rule according to the principles that the majority considers adequate. There is, in the long run, no such thing as an unpopular government maintaining a system that the multitude condemns as unfair. The rationale of representative government is not that majorities are God-like and infallible. It is the intent to bring about by peaceful methods the ultimately unavoidable adjustment of the political system and the men operating its steering mechanism to the ideology of the majority. The horrors of revolution and civil war can be avoided if a disliked government can be smoothly dislodged at the next election.

The true liberals firmly held that the market economy, the only economic system that warrants a steadily progressing improvement of mankind's material welfare, can work only in an atmosphere of undisturbed peace. They advocated government by the people's elected representatives because they took it for granted that only this system will lastingly preserve peace both in domestic and in foreign affairs.

What separated these true liberals from the blind majority-worship of the self-styled radicals was that they based their optimism concerning mankind's future not upon the mystic confidence in the infallibility of majorities but upon the belief that the power of sound logical argument is irresistible. They did not fail to see that the immense majority of common men are both too dull and too indolent to follow and to absorb long chains of reasoning. But they hoped that these masses, precisely on account of their dullness and indolence, could not help endorsing the ideas that the intellectuals brought to them. From the sound judgment of the cultured minority and from their ability to persuade the majority, the great leaders of the nineteenth-century liberal movement expected the steady improvement of human affairs.

In this regard there was full agreement between Carl Menger and his two earliest followers, Wieser and Böhm-Bawerk. Among the unpublished papers of Menger, Professor Hayek discovered a note that reads: "There is no better means to disclose the absurdity of a mode of reasoning than to let it pursue its full course to the end." All three of them liked to refer to Spinoza's argumentation in the first book of his *Ethics* that ends in the famous dictum, "*Sane sicut lux se ipsam et tenebras manifestat, sic veritas norma sui et falsi.*"[5] They looked calmly upon the passionate propaganda of both the Historical School and Marxism. They were fully convinced that the logically indefensible dogmas of these factions would eventually be rejected by all reasonable men precisely on account of their absurdity and that the masses of common men would necessarily follow the lead of the intellectuals.*

---

* There is need to add that Menger, Böhm-Bawerk, and Wieser looked with the utmost pessimism upon the political future of the Austrian Empire. But this problem cannot be dealt with in this essay.

5. "Indeed, just as light defines itself and darkness, so truth sets the standard for itself and falsity."

The wisdom of this mode of arguing is to be seen in the avoidance of the popular practice of playing off an alleged psychology against logical reasoning. It is true that often errors in reasoning are caused by the individual's disposition to prefer an erroneous conclusion to the correct one. There are even hosts of people whose affections simply prevent them from straight thinking. But it is a far cry from the establishment of these facts to the doctrines that in the last generation were taught under the label "sociology of knowledge." Human thinking and reasoning, human science and technology are the product of a social process insofar as the individual thinker faces both the achievements and the errors of his predecessors and enters into a virtual discussion with them either in assenting or dissenting. It is possible for the history of ideas to make understandable a man's failings as well as his exploits by analyzing the conditions under which he lived and worked. In this sense only is it permissible to refer to what is called the spirit of an age, of a nation, of a milieu. But it is circular reasoning if one tries to explain the emergence of an idea, still less to justify it, by referring to its author's environment. Ideas always spring from the mind of an individual, and history cannot say anything more about them than that they were generated at a definite instant of time by a definite individual. There is no other excuse for a man's erroneous thinking than what an Austrian Government once declared with regard to the case of a defeated general—that nobody is answerable for not being a genius. Psychology may help us to explain why a man failed in his thinking. But no such explanation can convert what is false into truth.

The Austrian economists unconditionally rejected the logical relativism implied in the teachings of the Prussian Historical School. As against the declarations of Schmoller and his followers, they maintained that there is a body of economic theorems that are valid for all human action irrespective of time and place, the national and racial characteristics of the actors, and their religious, philosophical, and ethical ideologies.

The greatness of the service these three Austrian economists have rendered by maintaining the cause of economics against the vain critique of Historicism cannot be overrated. They did not infer from their epistemological convictions any optimism concerning mankind's future evolution. Whatever is to be said in favor of correct logical thinking does not prove that the coming generations of men will surpass their ancestors in intellectual effort and achievements. History shows that again and again periods of marvelous mental accomplishments were followed by periods of decay and retrogression. We do not know whether the next generation will beget people who are able to continue along the lines of the geniuses who made the last centuries so glorious. We do not know anything about the biological conditions that enable a man to make one step forward in the march of intellectual advancement. We cannot preclude the assumption that there may be limits to man's further intellectual ascent. And certainly we do not know whether in this ascent there is not a point beyond which the intellectual leaders can no longer succeed in convincing the masses and making them follow their lead.

The inference drawn from these premises by the Austrian economists was, that while it is the duty of a pioneering mind to do all that his faculties enable him to perform, it is not incumbent upon him to propagandize for his ideas, still less to use questionable methods in order to make his thoughts palatable to people. They were not concerned about the circulation of their writings. Menger did not publish a second edition of his famous *Grundsätze*, although the book was long since out of print, second-hand copies sold at high prices, and the publisher urged him again and again to consent.

The main and only concern of the Austrian economists was to contribute to the advancement of economics. They never tried to win the support of anybody by other means than by the convincing power developed in their books and articles. They looked with indifference upon the fact that the universities of the German-speaking countries, even many of the Austrian universities, were hostile to economics as such and still more so to the new economic doctrines of subjectivism.

III

The Place of the Austrian School of Economics in the Evolution of Economics

1   The "Austrian School" and Austria

When the German professors attached the epithet "Austrian" to the theories of Menger and his two earliest followers and continuators, they meant it in a pejorative sense. After the battle of Königgrätz, the qualification of a thing as Austrian always had such a coloration in Berlin, that "headquarters of *Geist* [spirit, mind, intellect]," as Herbert Spencer sneeringly called it.* But the intended smear boomeranged. Very soon the designation "the Austrian School" was famous all over the world.

Of course, the practice of attaching a national label to a line of thought is necessarily misleading. Only very few Austrians—and for that matter, non-Austrians—knew anything about economics, and still smaller was the number of those Austrians whom one could call economists, however generous one might be in conferring this appellation. Besides, there were among the Austrian economists some who did not work along the lines which were called the "Austrian School"; best known among them were the mathematicians Rudolf Auspitz and Richard Lieben, and later Alfred Amonn and Josef Schumpeter. On the other hand, the number of foreign economists who applied themselves to the continuation of the work inaugurated by the "Austrians" was steadily increasing. At the beginning it sometimes happened that the endeavors of these British, American, and other non-Austrian economists met with opposition in their own countries and that they were ironically called "Austrians" by their critics. But after some years all

* Cf. Herbert Spencer, *The Study of Sociology*, 9th edition (London, 1880), p. 217.

the essential ideas of the Austrian School were by and large accepted as an integral part of economic theory. About the time of Menger's demise (1921), one no longer distinguished between an Austrian School and other economics. The appellation "Austrian School" became the name given to an important chapter of the history of economic thought; it was no longer the name of a specific sect with doctrines different from those held by other economists.

There was, of course, one exception. The interpretation of the causes and the course of the trade cycle which the present writer provided, first in his *Theory of Money and Credit** and finally in his treatise *Human Action†* under the name of the Monetary or Circulation Credit Theory of the trade cycle, was called by some authors the Austrian Theory of the trade cycle. Like all such national labels, this too is objectionable. The Circulation Credit Theory is a continuation, enlargement, and generalization of ideas first developed by the British Currency School and of some additions to them made by later economists, among them also the Swede, Knut Wicksell.

As it has been unavoidable to refer to the national label, "the Austrian School," one may add a few words about the linguistic group to which the Austrian economists belonged. Menger, Böhm-Bawerk, and Wieser were German Austrians; their language was German and they wrote their books in German. The same is true of their most eminent students—Johann von Komorzynski, Hans Mayer, Robert Meyer, Richard Schüller, Richard von Strigl, and Robert Zuckerkandl. In this sense the work of the "Austrian School" is an accomplishment of German philosophy and science. But among the students of Menger, Böhm-Bawerk, and Wieser there were also non-German Austrians. Two of them have distinguished themselves by eminent contributions, the Czechs Franz Čuhel and Karel Engliš.

2   The Historical Significance of the *Methodenstreit*

The peculiar state of German ideological and political conditions in the last quarter of the nineteenth century generated the conflict be-

---

* First German-language edition 1912, second German-language edition 1924. English-language editions 1934 and 1953. [Also Liberty Fund, 1980.]

† Yale University Press, 1949. [Also later English editions, Regnery, 1960; Foundation for Economic Education, 1996; Liberty Fund, 2007.]

tween two schools of thought out of which the *Methodenstreit* and the appellation "Austrian School" emerged. But the antagonism that manifested itself in this debate is not confined to a definite period or country. It is perennial. As human nature is, it is unavoidable in any society where the division of labor and its corollary, market exchange, have reached such an intensity that everybody's subsistence depends on other people's conduct. In such a society everybody is served by his fellow men, and in turn, he serves them. The services are rendered voluntarily: in order to make a fellow do something for me, I have to offer him something which he prefers to abstention from doing that something. The whole system is built upon this voluntariness of the services exchanged. Inexorable natural conditions prevent man from indulging in a carefree enjoyment of his existence. But his integration into the community of the market economy is spontaneous, the result of the insight that there is no better or, for that matter, no other method of survival open to him.

However, the meaning and bearing of this spontaneousness are only grasped by economists. All those not familiar with economics, i.e., the immense majority, do not see any reason why they should not by means of force coerce other people to do what these people are not prepared to do of their own accord. Whether the apparatus of physical compulsion resorted to in such endeavors is that of the government's police power or an illegal "picket" force whose violence the government tolerates, does not make any difference. What matters is the substitution of compulsion for voluntary action.

Due to a definite constellation of political conditions that could be called accidental, the rejection of the philosophy of peaceful cooperation was, in modern times, first developed into a comprehensive doctrine by subjects of the Prussian state. The victories in the three Bismarck wars had intoxicated the German scholars, most of whom were servants of the government. Some people considered it a characteristic fact that the adoption of the ideas of the Schmoller school was slowest in the countries whose armies had been defeated in 1866 and 1870. It is, of course, preposterous to search for any connection between the rise of the Austrian Economic Theory and the defeats, failures, and frustrations of the Habsburg regime. Yet, the fact that the French state universities kept out of the way of historicism and *Sozialpolitik* longer than those of other nations was certainly, at least to some extent, caused by the Prussian label attached to these doctrines. But this delay had little practical importance. France, like all other countries, became a stronghold of interventionism and proscribed economics.

The philosophical consummation of the ideas glorifying the government's interference, i.e., the action of the armed constables, was achieved by Nietzsche and by Georges Sorel. They coined most of the slogans that guided the butcheries of Bolshevism, Fascism, and Nazism. Intellectuals extolling the delights of murder, writers advocating censorship, philosophers judging the merits of thinkers and authors, not according to the value of their contributions but according to their achievements on battlefields,* are the spiritual leaders of our age of perpetual strife. What a spectacle was offered by those American authors and professors who ascribed the origin of their own nation's political independence and constitution to a clever trick of the "interests" and were casting longing glances at the Soviet paradise of Russia!

The greatness of the nineteenth century consisted in the fact that to some extent the ideas of Classical economics became the dominant philosophy of state and society. They transformed the traditional status society into nations of free citizens, royal absolutism into representative government, and above all, the poverty of the masses under the *ancien regime* into the well-being of the many under capitalistic laissez faire. Today the reaction of statism and socialism is sapping the foundations of Western civilization and well-being. Perhaps those are right who assert that it is too late to prevent the final triumph of barbarism and destruction. However this may be, one thing is certain. Society, i.e., peaceful cooperation of men under the principle of the division of labor, can exist and work only if it adopts policies that economic analysis declares as fit for attaining the ends sought. The worst illusion of our age is the superstitious confidence placed in panaceas which—as the economists have irrefutably demonstrated—are contrary to purpose.

Governments, political parties, pressure groups, and the bureaucrats of the educational hierarchy think they can avoid the inevitable consequences of unsuitable measures by boycotting and silencing the independent economists. But truth persists and works, even if nobody is left to utter it.

---

* Cf. the passages quoted by Julien Benda, *La trahison des clercs* (Paris, 1927), Note o, pp. 292–295. [English translation, *The Treason of the Intellectuals* (Wm. Morrow, 1928; Beacon Press, 1955).]

The typeface used in setting this book is Electra, designed in 1935 by the great American typographer William Addison Dwiggins. Dwiggins was a student and associate of Frederic Goudy and served for a time as acting director of Harvard University Press. In his illustrious career as typographer and book designer (he coined the term "graphic designer"), Dwiggins created a number of typefaces, including Metro and Caledonia, and designed as well many of the typographic ornaments or "dingbats" familiar to readers.

Electra is a crisp, elegant, and readable typeface, strongly suggestive of calligraphy. The contrast between its strokes is relatively muted, and it produces an even but still "active" impression in text. Interestingly, the design of the italic form—called "cursive" in this typeface—is less calligraphic than the italic form of many faces, and more closely resembles the roman.

This book is printed on paper that is acid-free and meets the requirements of the American National Standard for Permanence of Paper for Printed Library Materials, z39.48–1992. ∞

Book design adapted by Erin Kirk New, Watkinsville, Georgia, after a design by Martin Lubin Graphic Design, Jackson Heights, New York

Typography by Grapevine Publishing Services, LLC, Madison, Wisconsin

Printed and bound by Worzalla Publishing Company, Stevens Point, Wisconsin